A TRAMP ABOUT
THE WORLD

A TRAMP ABOUT
THE WORLD

PETER BIDDICK

NAVIGATOR BOOKS

Published by Navigator Books
Ringwood, Hampshire

Copyright © Peter Biddick 1994

ISBN 0 902830 24 4

Typeset by Moorhouse Typesetters
Printed at Alden Press Limited, Oxford and Northampton, Great Britain

This book is dedicated to
my wife Sue, also to that special breed
of men whose business takes them to
deep waters.

This story is about my sea going career from 1958 to 1964, mainly fact, with a bit of fiction added. It is not meant to upset anyone and if so, I apologise. I have never regretted going to sea and many a time in a difficult situation I will ask myself, what would I have done when I was in the Navy, and usually get a reasonable answer. When I tell my son about some of my experiences I had at sea when I was his age - 18 - he says, "Yes, but that was in the old days and things have changed." If they have changed that much I am sorry, as a lot of youngsters are missing out on a lot of life. Walking down the road the other day I bumped into an old friend of mine who is well into his 70's and spent his whole life at sea, a lot of the time as a bosun. He said to me "Peter, haven't we been lucky to have done the things we have and seen the sights we have." He was right and I consider myself a fortunate person to be able to recall some of the events that remain in my memory. Once someone has been to sea they will always have the taste of salt in their veins and will always have the love, and the fear of that vast spread of water until the day they die.

CONTENTS

Part One

Cadet

Part Two

Officer

Cover picture reproduced by kind permission of
FOTOFLITE, Littlestone Road,
New Romney, Kent TN28 8LN
and supplied by
Mr. BERT MOODY of the World Ship Society,
SOUTHAMPTON.

PART ONE

Chapter 1

Joining

The taxi stopped at the dockyard gate and the head of the security man peered into the back seat where I was sitting and asked what ship I was joining. I told him and he gave me a half sympathetic smile and told the driver to carry on. This was it! I was just 16 and heading for my first ship after doing 2 years training at a pre-sea school in North Wales. The school was for boys wishing to join the Royal or Merchant navies, mostly as seamen or in the engine room or stewards, but a few got qualified as officer cadets and I had been lucky enough to make the grade. It was a very tough establishment run on strict naval lines and some of the boys there were much to be desired and real hard cases, but I had survived and had left as a petty officer or prefect, if you prefer. The captain of the school was a man called George Washington Irwin, an enormous man whom all of the lads held in fear and awe, but in actual fact was a very fair and just man. It was only a couple of weeks ago that I had stood rigidly to attention in his office and he had said to me, "Biddick you have done well here and I have got you an apprenticeship with a great shipping company, so keep your nose clean and I am sure you will do well."

With his words going round in my brain I looked over the taxi driver's shoulder waiting for my first glance of the vessel from this great shipping company as we slowly picked our way through the chaos and confusion of the dock yard. At last we stopped at the bottom of a tall gangway, I paid the driver and took my suitcases out of the taxi and turned round to view my future home. The first thing I noticed were the rust stains running from the deck to the water line and she didn't have the bows of a destroyer to cut through the water, but a blunt bow that

1

looked like it wouldn't cut butter. I started climbing the very tall gangway and as the ship was empty it seemed to go up to the sky. When I got to the main deck I put my cases down, stood to attention, turned to the stern of the ship and gave a near perfect salute to what was supposed to be the Red ensign, but looked more like a red tatty rag. This is what I had been taught at training ship and I was sticking to it. I looked round for the officer of the day or one of the crew on gangway watch to repel boarders. Nobody. No one in sight, no sound of voices only the noise of a generator humming somewhere in the far distant beyond. I knew that it was a Sunday, but this was more like the 'Marie Celeste' than a hard working tramp steamer. Looking around all seemed chaos and dirty with the derricks at all different angles not as I expected them to be neatly fore and aft, hatch covers half on and half off and ropes and wires all over the place, not coiled down as taught at training school. All the paint work looked as though it could do with a good washing down and rusty streaks were all over the place. I peered down a half open hatch into the dark below and the smell that came up to greet me wasn't the most pleasant I had encountered. After a while I wandered past No. 3 hatch and looked up to the central accommodation with the bridge above. The bridge. Soon I would be up there waiting for crisp short orders from the Master or one of his officers as we cast off and sailed into the far beyond. That would be more like it. Feeling a bit more cheerful, I cast my eyes down from the bridge to the accommodation below and above the middle door was a white notice with the word Captain on it. Putting my cap on straight and brushing down my lovely doeskin uniform I decided to report to the Master of the vessel and started to climb the ladder to the next deck. Standing before the door I knocked gently waiting to meet the Captain and visualising a sort of Jack Hawkins type of man, to answer.

The door opened and before me stood a small man with a moustache, dark blue trousers, a string vest and wearing carpet slippers. There was also a very strong smell of Scotch. After my initial surprise I leapt to attention, gave a perfect salute and said in a much too loud voice, "Cadet Biddick reporting aboard sir", upon which he took half a pace back and I wasn't too sure who was the most surprised. He looked me up and down once and then once more to make sure he wasn't seeing things, then scratching his hairy chest with one hand, he held out his other hand and shaking my hand he said "Nice to see you aboard Biddick, your first ship I assume", with a glint in his eye. Not very nautical I thought and definitely not the Jack Hawkins type. "Yes sir, my first ship" I replied, not knowing whether another salute was in order but deciding against it. He gave a loud burp and the definite aroma of Scotch headed my way as he said, "Go and find the 3rd Mate and he will show you your cabin and put you right, I will see you later." The door shut in my face before my right hand even thought of a salute.

I went down to the main deck, my suitcase bumping behind me, to try and find the 3rd's cabin, but as there was still no sign of life around I started to walk up the alleyways to find my bearings. At last I came to a cabin with 1st Officer above the door so I must be getting warm and sure enough next to that was a cabin with 2nd Officer and then, bingo, the 3rd Mate's cabin. I stood outside the tightly closed door and listened. I heard a sort of groaning coming from within. What on earth was happening? Oh well, I thought, in for a penny in for a pound and nervously tapped on the wooden door. "Oh Christ, who in the hell is that?" shouted the voice from within. "Cadet Biddick reporting aboard sir" I replied in a small tone. "Come in, come in" said the voice and I opened the door not knowing what to expect. I stepped into the cabin and looked around the small steel white space trying to see the owner of the voice. There, laying on the bunk, was a man with his trousers around his ankles and he seemed to have his hand up his bottom! "Sodding piles" he moaned, "it's this bloody damp ship", as he applied some sort of cream up his backside. As I hadn't heard of piles it was all beyond me, so I decided to give him a salute and said "Yes sir." "Cut out all that bullshit" he said, swinging himself off his bunk and pulling his trousers up. He gave me the once up and down and with a half smile on his face said "Your cabin is the one next door, go and stow your gear. The senior cadet is on leave, but will be back tomorrow and he will show you the ropes. I will see you in the saloon tonight for dinner, so go and get out of your lovely new uniform and get into some working gear" he said. I backed towards the cabin door realising that I was being dismissed, I mumbled "Yes sir." "Look" he said fairly friendly, "just call me third or mister and save all your sirs for the Captain, now push off." I stepped out of the cabin and closed the door quickly behind me. It all seemed very odd to me that all the standing to attention and saluting that I had been taught in the training ship didn't seem to apply to this ship. Oh well, I thought and picked up my suitcases and walked along to the next door which had the sign 'Cadets' over it and opened it to see my new home.

It was very similar to the cabin I had just left except it had two bunks, but it was still small, steel, painted a sort of white and also smelt damp. It had a table bolted to the deck, a couple of chairs, a nice round brass porthole, and lockers, a couple of which were open and empty so I assumed that they were for me. I changed out of my uniform and got into my working gear, a set of brand new blues, and set-to to stow all my clothing, navigation books, seamanship books and all my personal effects into the lockers. It started off all in neat piles, but after a while I realised that it wouldn't all fit in like that and in the end it was a job of just stuffing it all in. When I had finished, to the best of my ability, I sat down and had a think about what I had learnt about

4

life afloat so far. I knew that saluting was out and I wasn't too sure about my uniform, but this I couldn't understand as I was sure that most of my time would be on the bridge working out the ship's position, giving orders here, giving orders there and generally being an officer. God, how wrong I was! The cadet, I got to know in a very short time, was the lowest of the low, not an officer, not a seaman, but sort of in limbo, given the dirtiest, smelliest nastiest jobs on board, a true training to any job when told. But at this point in time I was as innocent as a virgin.

As nobody had given me any instructions of what to do, I laid down on the bunk and had a snooze, to be awakened by a knock on the door and the 3rd Mate coming in. "Settling in?" he said as he sprawled himself into one of the chairs. I jumped off the bunk and sort of stood to attention and he waved me into the chair opposite him. We started chatting and I asked him about the ship and he explained that she was built in 1937, making her the grand old age of 21, she was 3,600 tons gross, a length of 401 feet with a breadth of 53 feet. The engines were steam reciprocating that should give her a speed of 10½ knots with the wind behind and if they didn't break down he said with a grin. The officers and crew came to about 30 in all and he said that the crew were a real hard lot as the ship was so old and tatty it was the best they could get and a lot of the seamen had bad discharges from other ships and were trouble.

The 3rd Mate said his name was Mike and he had served his time with the company and had got his 2nd Mate's ticket earlier in the year and was hoping to move to a better shipping company at the end of the next trip. He was about 21 and was going for his 1st Mate's ticket in a years time.

Looking at his watch he got up and, as he was leaving, turned and said he would see me in the saloon in half an hour for dinner which he explained was at the end of the alleyway, past No. 3 hatch and into the main accommodation housing. After he departed I got changed into my best uniform again. Another mistake. I was looking forward to my dinner, to be waited on by the stewards, all silver service, of course. The food at the naval school hadn't been too bad, but I was sure that the food served to Merchant navy officers must be the best, just like on the cruise liners. Having given my shoes a good cleaning and brushed down my uniform I made my way down the alleyway and out on to the main deck, passing the hatch and into the main housing. I passed the galley on my right hand side and was surprised to hear two girls giggling and one saying to the other "Oh, isn't he lovely and so young." I knew they must be talking about me and I thought it was nice to have some females on board and that could make life more interesting. Wrong! It didn't take long to find out that my two young girls happened to be a couple of stewards and true blue fairies, but thank God they kept themselves to themselves. Taking my cap off and placing it under my arm I made my entrance into the saloon and stood stiffly to attention by the door. The conversation that had been going on came to an abrupt end and every face was pointing in my direction and a voice said, "F--- me, its midshipman Easy." "Belay that" growled a voice from the head of the table, and I recognised that the Captain had spoken. The talk continued and one of the stewards (or stewardesses) ushered me to one of the empty chairs next to the 3rd Mate, and I sat down. Looking around I noticed that not one person was actually wearing a uniform and most were wearing blue working reefer jackets, some white shirts, some in boiler suits who I assumed must be the engineers, and the Captain who was at least wearing a uniform jacket, but it didn't look as though it had been cleaned for about 10 years and the four gold rings that denoted his rank on his arm looked like mildew.

The saloon had a top table at which sat the Captain, 1st Mate and Chief Engineer, and two tables running from it of which it seemed that the deck officers sat at one and the engineering officers at the other thus ensuring that water and oil never mix. Behind where the Captain sat was the forward bulkhead with three portholes in it looking out on to No. 2 hatch and on to the forecastle of the ship. Up minced one of the stewards and asked if I would like soup and upon my asking what was the soup of the day I was told Brown Windsor and it would be the soup of the day until the cook ran out of it. We never seemed to run out of it! It turned up with a nice coating of grease over it, the main course - pork chops - had a nice covering of grease and even the creme caramel and coffee to follow, had traces of grease. So my dreams of great meals disappeared out of the porthole and the meals on that ship never took a turn for the better and the mad cook and 2nd cook, always covered in grease, continued to try to give us all ulcers. I know that the shipping company had a reputation of hungry by name and hungry by nature, and over the next four years I could sure vouch for it.

After dinner I retired back to my cabin and once more took off my lovely new uniform, brushed it down, hung it up and realised that it was redundant. Having nothing else to do I read for an hour then wandered down the alleyway to find the heads and washroom and found it just as dank and cold as I expected.

Laying in my bunk I wondered if it had been an omen that the previous night I had been to the cinema to see "A night to remember", all about the sinking of the Titanic! Today had been a strange day and not in the slightest what I had expected or been prepared for, and as for tomorrow? At least I would have some company as the senior cadet was back and he would give me some idea of what to do and what not to do.

I was awakened at about 2am by an almighty noise coming from the 3rd Mate's cabin, but in the morning I found out their was nothing to worry about. It was only some of the crew coming back aboard after a night on the booze, didn't like the 3rd

Mate so they put a fire axe through his door and tried to beat him up!

And so ended my first day in the Merchant Navy.

Chapter 2

First Trip

It was September and the weather was turning chilly with a low mist hanging over the docks at Hull. As I made my way to the saloon for breakfast I gave a little shiver and hoped that in a couple of days we would be heading for warmer climes and a bit of warm sun. This dream disappeared rapidly when I asked the 3rd Mate where we were heading. "Back up bloody north again" he snorted, "back to all the charms of the Hudson Bay and Port Churchill and the joys of the North Atlantic at this time of the year." Not too sure where the Hudson Bay was, when I got back to my cabin I got out my old school atlas and found that the 3rd was right and it was a long way north, about latitude 60°, just short of the Arctic Circle, passing Greenland to starboard, through the Hudson Straits with Baffin Island also to starboard then on to Port Churchill. Delving into another book all I could find out about the Hudson Bay was that it was only open from mid July to October. I wondered what date it shut in October as it was now September and time was marching on!

About 9.30 the senior cadet burst into the cabin and introduced himself as he got changed out of his civilian clothes and into his working clothes. His name was Ken and he was in his third year as a cadet and next year would be sitting his 2nd Mate's ticket and, as he said, saying goodbye to this wondrous shipping company and moving to better things. He took me with him to introduce me to the Chief Officer who then told us to report to the bosun for instructions of what job he wanted us to do as we were preparing to sail later on in the day. For the next few hours it was all rush and tear and I worked with Ken on various jobs. Our first task was working with a couple of crew, to swing the top beams into the hatches and get them covered.

The old steam winches, belching out steam in all directions, lifted the heavy beams off the main deck, over the open hatches and we guided them into position, then on went the wooden hatch covers and finally we stretched out two or three canvas tarpaulins. They were then secured by long lengths of metal called locking bars and secured by wooden wedges which we knocked in with hammers. Nowadays to cover a hatch a button is pressed and it is all done automatically. The ship had five hatches and as we finished each one, the bosun followed us with another team and lowered the derricks down to a horizontal position and secured them for sea.

All was activity, with stores being swung aboard, the fresh water tanks being filled, dockers who had done some jobs clearing up and going ashore and some of the shipping office persons getting forms filled in and then getting off in a hurry, I assumed not wanting to be hijacked. After lunch the Chief Officer told me to check the whole ship to see if any stowaways were aboard. God, I thought, who in their right mind would want to stow away on this rust bucket! But this was a job I had to do before leaving each port and at least it gave me a chance to have a look around. I started in the bows, down in the chain locker where the anchor chain was coiled down, a place I got to hate as it was one of the plum jobs that the cadets had to paint it with red lead. From the chain locker I started on the holds and had to climb down into the pitch black, armed with a weak torch, check the tween decks, then down to the main hold. It was big, empty, dark and eerie and if I had met anyone mad enough to be down there I am sure I would have had a heart attack. I worked my way through all the holds to the stern and emerged into the daylight and then on to the crew's quarters, to make certain that they hadn't smuggled any females aboard. It was pretty tatty in the accommodation and I got some funny looks from the crew who were in there and told in very straight language to go away.

From the crew's quarters I next went into the steering flat which is the place that the steering gear is connected to the rudder and the other way up to the steering wheel on the bridge. It was quite a complex piece of machinery, all pistons and things, and I found out later that in the crew's section it was very noisy with that moving around all over the place. What with that and the propeller below the rudder to try and get some peace in a rough sea it must have been hell, especially in a nice gale when the prop came out of the sea and raced like mad.

From the stern the next stop was the engine room and down into the bowels of the vessel, the very heart. To me the first time down there the engines looked enormous and I didn't fancy the thought of being stuck down there for eight hours a day with the smell of oil and grease all around. At least on deck you could get some fresh air and the occasional bit of sun, but down here... The engineers seemed to love it and I don't think that I ever saw an engineer sun bathing, but it was them that kept the engines going, or most of the time. Each to their own I thought as I half walked and half crawled along the prop shaft tunnel which ran from the engine room to the stern of the ship and the point where the prop shaft was joined to the prop itself. It must be fun doing this with the prop shaft turning ten to a dozen.

I emerged from the engine room and looked at my check list and saw the last place to look was the lifeboats. I climbed up to the lifeboat deck and after undoing the cover hoisted myself into one of our life saving devices. Sitting on a thwart I guessed what it must be like to be cast adrift in one surrounded by about twelve hairy seaman in a force 9 and mountainous seas. Having put the cover back on I walked away not wishing to dwell on those kind of thoughts.

At last the hubbub on the ship seemed to be dying down as I reported back to the 1st Officer that to the best of my knowledge we had not aliens aboard. It was smoko time (tea

11

break) so I joined some of the seamen sitting on one of the hatches and was told that we were waiting for the pilot to come aboard. My duties, Ken informed me, during the operation of getting under way were on the bridge, operating the ships telegraph and keeping the movement book, which was a record of orders given and the times. Half an hour before we sailed, Ken and I had to go to the bridge and test the telegraph and ship's whistle, to make sure nothing fell off or got stuck, I thought ruefully.

About 20 minutes later a man with a long blue raincoat came up the gangway and asked the directions to the Captain's cabin. The pilot was with us, and told us to be ready to take a tug's line in about half an hour. Ken and I made our way up to the bridge to do our testing. It was the first time I had been to the bridge and it all seemed very small with the main wheelhouse in the centre and open wings each side, but it did seem a long way up from the water line as I peered over the side of the wing. The wheelhouse itself was very cramped with the Captain's chair in one corner and the compass housing and binnacle taking up much of the room. No radar in sight, much too old for that, as were telephones but contact to the engine room and the Captain's cabin were maintained by good old fashioned brass speaking tubes! Orders to the bows and the stern were passed on by a lovely brass megaphone. the windows in the bridge looked like they had been taken off some old steam train, the type with a heavy leather strap to lower them and the ones that couldn't be opened had sets of windscreen wipers on them that could serve just as well on a Morris Minor. There was one telegraph on each wing of the bridge, covered by canvas hoods and when we uncovered them the brass gleamed and this I found out was by way of the cadets. Ken told me to go up the monkey island, which was an open deck above the bridge, to raise the "H" flag to inform anyone that might be interested that we had a pilot aboard. It was open and exposed up there and the only thing to bump into was the DF hoop (direction finder) and not much else, apart from the secondary steering position, which was a smaller version of the binnacle on the bridge. It must have been lovely to stand up there, exposed to all the elements, trying to steer. I climbed back down to the bridge and into the wheelhouse and saw Ken blowing into the brass pipe marked engine room and a voice floated up and said "Yes". "Ready to test telegraphs?" Ken asked and the voice came back and replied "Yes". Chatty lot I thought as we moved out to the wing of the bridge. With a sweaty hand I got hold of the cold brass handle, Ken nodded and I moved the handle from finished with engines right back to full astern to full ahead. Dring dring, it went, then lo and behold the small repeater handle went dring dring and followed my indicator to full ahead. Half ahead to half astern, slow ahead to slow astern we went through all the movements with the engine room indicator obediently following with its dring drings. Wonderful I thought, we have actual contact with the engines. Ken once more puffed down the tube to check all was okay with them, got the usual "Yes" and the tube cover shut. Next to check was the ship's whistle and I was told to give the lanyard a couple of yanks. Looking astern to the funnel I swung on the lanyard and saw a steam emitting from the whistle in all directions and then a deep throated BOO. This is power, I mused and gave it a longer tug, thinking what a lovely sound, but as time went on I learned to detest it as when the ship ran into fog, day or night, we had to sound our whistle every few minutes to let other ships in the area know that we were about, and after a few days of that it did tend to wear one down.

"All okay" said Ken, "give the old man a buzz and say all is well, I'm off to the bows as that's my station for leaving harbour, see you later" and he went off down the bridge ladder. I made my way to the tube marked Captain and gave a nervous puff down it. I heard the cover come off the other end and a voice saying "Well?". "Bridge gear tested sir" I said down the tube. "Very well" came the reply "I'll be up in a few minutes". Walking out to the bridge wing I looked over the dodgers and saw that a tug was nestling alongside the bows and a rope was being attached to it by a couple of seamen. The Chief Officer was up there as were the carpenter, who looked after the windlass, a couple more seamen and Ken was just joining them to take in some of our ropes and wires from the dock so that we finished up with just one bow rope and one spring. Looking astern the same operation was in progress with the 2nd Mate in charge of that end.

I walked back into the wheelhouse and saw that one of the seamen had got behind the steering wheel and was testing it by putting it to hard a port then hard a starboard and checking that the wheel indicator was responding. He gave a wink as I walked past and said "Okay mate" and I smiled and nodded. At that moment the 3rd Mate appeared at a run, gave the helmsman a dirty look and went into the chart room with the helmsman giving him a two fingered salute behind his back. The Captain and the pilot appeared and went out to the landside of the bridge to see what state we were in to get under way. "Stand by engines" he said looking at me and I went to the telegraph and rang it to the stand by position and putting down the time in the bridge movement book. Dring dring went my friend. The 3rd Mate came out of the chart room and stood by the wheelhouse door to relay orders to the helmsman and myself and also armed himself with the megaphone to yell orders to the bows and stern. We had now singled up to just the bow rope and the stern line and the tug was taking the strain at the bows. The pilot said "Let go astern", and the 3rd Mate screamed the order through the megaphone in the general direction of the stern. God knows what happens in a strong wind I thought, the 2nd Mate would never hear. The win was blowing us off the dock so as the bow rope was ordered to be cast off, and the men on the quay let the rope fall into the water, we moved easily away from the dockside with the tug giving us a gentle haul. "Slow ahead" said the pilot and dring dring went my telegraph, and I felt the ship begins to shudder as the prop bit into the water and we slowly moved ahead passing a ship that was tied up ahead of me. Goodbye England, I said to myself and was quite excited with the whole situation. The Captain, during the getting under way operation, had prowled up and down the bridge keeping an eye on things as it is an odd situation with a pilot on board. The pilot gives the orders and is in charge, but if the situation arose that the Captain thought that the ship was in danger he could over rule the pilot and take over.

We moved out slowly from the dock and turned down the river Humber heading for Spurn Head at the entrance of the river. Once clear of the dock I saw that the seamen on the bows let the tug go and with a couple of toots it head back to its base having done its job. As we steamed slowly down the river, the Captain told me to get hold of a seaman and put the pilot ladder over the ship's side. I went down to the main deck and collared a seaman to give me a hand to tie the pilot ladder to the ship's rail and lower it down until it was just above the water line. I saw the pilot cutter charging through the water towards us at a great rate of knots and as I heard the sound of the telegraph and the ship slowed down, the cutter came alongside just below the ladder. The pilot turned up alongside me, said "See you" swung his legs over the rails and climbed down the ladder and jumped on to his launch and with a wave went into the cockpit, his job over. Today the sea was flat, but I have seen pilots doing that operation in a strong wind and heavy seas and then it becomes very dangerous with the chance of a man getting crushed between the ship's side and the launch. With the small boat leaping all over the place and the pilot trying to jump off the rope ladder on to its deck, they then earn their money. The funny thing was that I never saw an accident.

After pulling the ladder up on to the deck and rolling it up I returned to the bridge and was surprised to note that the land was on our starboard side which meant that we were heading south not in the general direction of Canada. I went into the chart room and asked the 3rd Mate about this and he told me that we were first going to Flushing in the Netherlands to pick up bunkers, oil, before going north. Long way to go for just a bit of oil I thought, but I supposed that it was cheaper there. The Chief Officer turned up and said that I would be on the 4-8 watch which meant that I was on duty from 4am until 8am then from 4pm to 8pm, but he said that I would be working extra hours as the bilges would need cleaning and the chippy would need a hand to get the shifting boards ready for our cargo of grain. Shifting boards, I found out later, were to stop the cargo of grain from moving thus giving us a list, thus stopping us from turning over. Good idea, I thought. I didn't really relish the idea of going on watch at 4am, but I was there to do as I was ordered.

As the time now was 5pm I was now on watch and the 3rd Mate told me to report to the bosun and give a hand to stow the ropes and wires away and help with the washing down of the decks and generally clear the decks. When I had done this and other jobs I returned to the bridge where I was told to stand lookout on the wing of the bridge and report any ship or, as it was getting dark, any lights of other vessels. The Captain was also on the bridge as it was the 3rd Mate's watch and, as he was the youngest watch officer, the Captain liked to hang around. After about half an hour I had driven the poor 3rd mad as I reported lights to him that were just on the horizon and miles away. He told me to behave myself and use my common sense and I heard a chuckle from a dark shape slumped in the Captain's chair. After a while the 3rd stopped his pacing of the bridge and told me to relive the helmsman and have a go at the wheel. He stood behind me as I took the spokes of the wheel in my hands and peeped at the dimly lit compass. I was told the course and after a few minutes to get the feel of it I kept her on a pretty straight course. We had had quite a bit of steering practice at the training school, but this was the real thing with the ship moving under me and a gentle roll. After about three quarters of an hour the helmsman, who had been standing behind me just in case I decided to head the ship towards land, took over again. "Well done Biddick", said the Captain from his chair, "not bad for the first trick at the wheel." High praise indeed, and I walked back to the wing with a spring in my step.

At 20.00 I was relieved in my duty as lookout by a young seaman and that was the end of my first watch and I departed the bridge and made my way down to my cabin. Ken was there and he told me that the Chief Officer had put him on day work this trip which meant that he didn't have to stand watches, but work sort of office hours 08.00 to 17.00. He brought us a couple of cups of coffee from the galley and we had a long chinwag about ourselves and I asked a lot of questions about a lot of things I still didn't understand about the ship and its way of life. At about 22.30 I got ready to turn into my bunk as I was to be given a call at 03.45 to get on watch at 04.00. God! did a time like that exist!

Yes it did! From deep in my sleep I felt a hand on my shoulder and being shaken and a voice saying "Time to get up mate, you're on watch in fifteen minutes." I swung my legs over the side of my bunk after switching on my bunk light and started putting on some warm clothing. From the other side of the cabin I heard Ken snoring gently and thought, lucky sod. I grabbed my duffle coat and wedged on one of my old hats and after switching off the light stepped out of the fairly warm cabin into the not so

17

warm alleyway. I headed up to the bridge even though I was about five minutes early. One of the biggest crimes on a ship is to be late to relieve some one on watch and I have seen murder nearly committed with a person who is persistently late. After standing on the bridge for four hours, especially at night, the only thing you want to do is get off it and relax and for every five minutes that you remain there after your stint it feels like five hours. Walking up and down the wing of the bridge was the lookout, rubbing his hands together to try and get some warmth into them as after an hour up there it got pretty cold. He pointed out to me the position of the relevant shipping lights and then scuttled off to his warm bunk. The 2nd Mate was handing over to the 3rd, showing him the ship's position on the chart and the state of the ships that were in our vicinity and any that could be a problem. I must admit that when I was sailing as 2nd Mate I used to like the 12-4 watch, or as it is called the graveyard watch, as it was peaceful with most of the crew and officers tucked up in their bunks, including the skipper. The 2nd came out of the wheelhouse, closing the sliding door behind him to keep what little warmth there was in, and left the bridge with a smile to me and a "Goodnight."

The watch continued and I was summoned to go on the wheel again for the last hour and even had to alter course for a couple of ships under the close watch of the 3rd Mate. The sun made a watery appearance at about 07.30 as did the Captain. He was still wearing his old jacket and looked as though he needed a good shave and as he walked up and down I could still get the aroma of Scotch about him. At 08.00 my relief turned up to take over the wheel and I departed the bridge to have a wash, then breakfast. Over my greasy eggs I found out that we would be docking at Flushing at about noon, but no shore leave as we would be taking on our oil then straight back off to sea again.

After breakfast I reported to the Chief Officer, as he was the one in charge of all that goes on on the deck, and he allocated the jobs that had to be done around the ship. Each morning the bosun reported to him and the days working programme was sorted out as were the problems. This morning I was to give Ken a hand to check the two lifeboats and make sure that the emergency rations hadn't been stolen and that the freshwater tanks hadn't sprung a leak and, if possible, try and start the motor that was in one of them. Once a week we had lifeboat practice when at sea, when everyone that wasn't on watch assembled at the lifeboat stations, but it all seemed a bit of a farce as members of the crew sauntered to their positions, some with life jackets, some without, and we never actually swung the boats out and I had this horrible feeling that if they ever left the safety of their chocks they would collapse. At these practices the crew used to moan like hell and mumble, waste of f------ time. Still, I'm pleased that we never put them to the test.

As I sat in the port lifeboat checking the emergency stores it was quite pleasant to watch the water slip past the hull way down on the water line and to see the different types of ships around us as it was getting fairly busy as we approached the southern tip of Holland. Flushing was at the entrance to the Wester Schelde which runs on to Antwerp, about another 30 miles up the river and, as it's a very busy port, there was a lot of shipping around. Checking the stores I thought that anyone on a diet would love to be cast adrift in our lifeboat and would soon lose pounds. After a lot of cursing Ken came to the conclusion that the engine didn't want to start and we would have to get one of the engineers up to sort it out, but at a later date. The 3rd Mate yelled down to us from the bridge to cover up the lifeboats and get the log in. The ship's log, not the one that got written in, was at the stern of the ship. It consisted of a dial enclosed in a brass casing which was fixed to the stern rail and attached to

19

that was a long length of line which was cast into the sea behind the ship. At the other end of the line was a brass torpedo shaped object with fins attached and as the ship went through the water it rotated. The brass dial on the ship gave a reading of how many miles we were doing per hour and each day at noon it was one of my jobs to take the reading and report it to the officers who were working out the ship's position and, if it wasn't possible to take a sun sight, you had to work out a dead reckoning position which consisted of the log's reading and the state of the wind and drift. With a bit of luck you could find out where you were.

By the time we had the log in and stowed away I saw that the Dutch pilot was approaching in his cutter and when he climbed up the ladder, and on to the deck, I ushered him up to the bridge, where I stayed for going alongside our berth. The fuelling jetty was miles from anywhere and was one long pier with lots of fuel lines ready to fill up its hungry customers. We got alongside with only one panic when the engines decided not to work, but we had two very large Dutch tugs to get us out of trouble and those men knew what they were doing. As soon as we had our bow and stern ropes out the large fuel lines came aboard and started to fill our tanks and we had the lovely smell of diesel all around the ship. The chippy ran a water line from the jetty and topped up the fresh water and I had to give him a hand to dip the tanks and make sure that they were full to the brim.

One of the derricks was hoisted and the old steam winch swung a couple of pallets of stores aboard and also some bonded goods which included beer, cigarettes and, I noticed, quite a few cases of Scotch, which I assumed was the old man's life line. We had to give a hand to stow them away in lock up store under the watchful eye of the chief steward to make sure that the cases of beer all arrived and none went walkabout.

After about four hours we were all ready to cast off and with the help of our Dutch tugs we slipped away from the jetty and headed back to the sea and towards the English Channel. As luck would have it I was back on watch and as the deck boy, one of the watch, didn't know how to steer I had a two hour trick on the wheel, but it was interesting as we had to dodge around quite a few ships and time soon went. When I was relieved the 3rd Mate told me to go below on stand by and, if I was needed, he had a whistle to blow to summon me to the bridge. As it was Sunday the next day and the Captain gave the ship an inspection each Sunday, he suggested that I made sure that my cabin was clean and ship-shape, also the wash room and heads that we used. I left the bridge and stood on the deck leaning over the rails and as we were now rolling quite nicely I enjoyed looking out and seeing the sky one moment and then peering down into the depths of the ocean the next. As we were light, we were rolling like a pig, but the funny thing was that I didn't feel sea sick at all and I have been very lucky and never suffered with it at all. I have seen some people at sea who have really been ill and just wish they could die and some who have been at sea all their lives still suffer for a while until they get their sea legs. I must be odd because I stood there and thought, this is it, this is what going to sea is all about.

And so we started to settle into a routine as we crawled down the Channel with a west wind on our nose and doing about eight knots. I found that getting up at 03.45 was tiring and as us cadets had quite a lot of overtime to do, as well as our studying each day, it was nice to crash out on our bunks. One of the main jobs that we had to do was the joy of bilge cleaning which once again the lucky cadets were selected to do. The last trip she had been up in Churchill and had brought back a cargo of grain so we had the pleasure of crawling through the bilges with buckets and scooping out the wet grain that had seeped into them. It wasn't

21

very nice being stuck in the bowels of the ship with the only light in the dark hatches being clusters and the ship rolling and pitching all over the place. It stank down there and we got filthy each time we went down and so it was washing our clothes each day as well as all the other jobs. A couple of seamen worked with us and we slowly worked through each hatch until they were all clear, and to the bosun's standard. The bosun was a 6' 4" giant of a man from the Scottish Isles and one day I made the mistake of disagreeing with him over some point or other and the next moment I felt the full force of the palm of his hand round my ear. Another lesson learnt! He was a very good seaman and had the unenviable job of keeping the crew in order of which they weren't the best on this God's earth, but he was big enough to handle himself.

As we didn't have an auto pilot on the ship there had to be a man on the wheel the whole time so that half my watch was steering and the other half on look out, cleaning the brass work on the bridge, other small jobs and making the tea. The steering part nearly caused a mutiny and that day I definitely wasn't the flavour of the month! We had just rounded southern Ireland and were heading towards northern Canada on a nice day but with long Atlantic rollers hitting our bows but not causing her to roll too much. It was about 07.45 and I had been on the wheel for some time and my mind was wandering and I was thinking about breakfast when I went off watch and other things. I looked down at the compass and saw we were quite a bit off course so I tried to correct her by putting a lot of port helm on. Too much I thought as I saw the compass needle whip past our correct course and put the wheel hard a starboard to try and correct her. After a few minutes of the ship going through the water like a drunken duck I managed to get those large Atlantic rollers beam on and did we roll as I started to get the ship to turn a full circle! As we were beam on and she was rolling about 45% I heard crashes and curses coming from the galley and found out later that all the pots and pans and breakfast had finished up in a corner on the deck. Up to the bridge came the Captain at full gallop and out of the chart room came the 3rd Mate at the same speed just as I had managed to get the ships bows pointing towards dear old England! After the panic had settled down and we were back on the true course, and I had my fortune told me by two very angry officers, the cook appeared on the bridge waving a very large ladle and what he was going to do with it to me wasn't worth thinking about. Breakfast that day, when I eventually got it, was a very sober affair.

We plodded on north and the weather was getting colder and it seemed like we were in permanent gales. During one of these gales the steering gear went wrong and we lay wallowing for two hours whilst the engineers put it right and then about twenty four hours later the engines stopped and it took some eighteen hours to sort that out. I didn't envy the poor engineers stuck down in the bowels of the ship while we rolled on our beam ends and they were doing their repairs. I know that once I was in my bunk it was rolling so much that I got flung out and finished up in a heap on the deck and trying to eat at a table in the saloon was nigh enough impossible. Everyone gave a heartfelt cheer when we heard the sound of the engines getting under way once more and at least we had our bows into the vile weather and didn't roll quite so much. A couple of times the tarpaulins on the forward hatches got blown open and we had to make our way to them holding on to the life lines that had been fixed up and, with the wind shrieking round us, replace them and secure the fixing bars and hammer in the wooden blocks again.

Each day I had to do about one and a half hours studying and I had been given my 4 year syllabus by the Captain after we had left Flushing. It covered many subjects such as ships construction, navigation, principles of navigation, rules of the road, safety, fire fighting, signals, and much more. After doing my sea time I would have to go to college for about 3 months to sit my 2nd Mates ticket and the actual exam lasted a week ending with an oral exam which could last one and a half hours and you can be asked any question on the sea and regulations, which covered a vast range. I plugged away at it and at least when I got stuck on a question or a point I could ask Ken or one of the mates and they were all helpful.

After 17 days the faint outline of land appeared on our port bow and I was told it was Newfoundland and we were approaching the entrance to the Hudson Straits and then into the Hudson Bay. It had taken a long time to get this far as the weather had been appalling and at times the wind had been so strong the Captain had ordered slow ahead so that the ship didn't actually break up. Not only did we have strong winds but we encountered quite a bit of fog, and when fog was around I had the pleasure of standing lookout on the bows. After an hour of standing up there with freezing fog all around you it wasn't a bundle of fun. If you spotted anything you had to ring the bell and indicate to the bridge the direction of the sighting. We encountered a few icebergs drifting silently past us and it is true that you can sense and smell ice when it's about. Dangerous things, and even with radar they are difficult to spot especially bergy bits, which are small icebergs, and the radar doesn't always pick them up, so a good set of eyes on lookout is very necessary. Some of the bergs were gigantic and even a few miles off they looked like gigantic cathedrals and the thing that always got me was the silence that went with them.

We passed through the straits with Baffin Island on our starboard side, then the Islands of Salisbury, Nottingham and Coates before entering the bay. I didn't realise how big the Hudson Bay was, but when I asked how far to Churchill and was told to work it out on the chart it worked out that it was about another 550 miles to go. It is a very big bay! At 10 knots, with the weather kind, another two and a half days to get there. The weather had flattened a bit and we got a few glimpses of a very watery sun and that night I saw the most wonderful display of the northern lights, the Aurora Borealis, with the whole of the night sky ablaze with lights. A most remarkable sight and one I won't forget. During the next day, with the weather still kind to us, we got some fine views of Beluga whales as they played around in the water and to see those giants nearly leaping out of the water was quite something. I found out later that it was one of their breeding grounds and that it was a big tourist attraction for Churchill, as there wasn't much else to entice people there. As we approached Churchill the weather took a definite turn for the worst and for the next twenty four hours we had to steam up and down outside the port as it was too rough to anchor, and no way could a pilot board ship as she pitched and rolled all over the place. Looking towards the shore it was very flat with the great silos sticking out and a few buildings surrounding it, and not much else. After doing my spell at the wheel I went below, pretty boring having to just keep going up and down outside the harbour, and joined the 2nd Mate for a beer and a chat. He had been to Churchill a few times and knew quite a bit about the place and launched into his tourist guide speech. Churchill, it seemed, had no roads out of it and the only way to leave was to fly out or go by train, of which there was three trains a week. It was one of the largest grain ports in the world and also called polar bear city as this was another attraction. If one wished you could go on conducted tours to see the bears, but this time of the year they did tend to enter town to see what they could get in the way of food so, he said, when ashore, keep ones eyes open for the stray bear. I thought he was joking, but he wasn't! The population of Churchill was about 1,300 and many of those were Inuits of which quite a few worked at the silos. The main store was the Hudson Bay Trading Company which opened up there about 250 years ago, mainly for the fur trade and across the entrance to the river was a fort called Prince of Wales Fort which was built to protect the Hudson Bay Company and constructed in about 1700. Winnipeg was 1,000 miles away by train. He finished his lecture by saying that the temperature got down to about 40° minus. Not a very nice place, I thought, and hoped to God that we got out before we got frozen in and had to spend the winter here.

The weather eased off and we edged our way closer in and the radio officer informed the Captain that the pilot was on his way out to us, and when he was safely on board took us up to our landing berth under one of the giant silos. It was very nice to move the telegraph handle to "finished with engines" when we were securely tied up and we all thanked God that the prop had stayed on and we had all got here in one piece. The quietness was odd as was the fact that we weren't all being flung all over the place and you could walk along a flat deck without holding on for dear life. We would start loading tomorrow so that at least we would all have a few hours peace and have a run ashore in the evening and explore this outback of humanity, and best of all get a full nights sleep in my bunk. After lunch, which made a change for most of the officers to eat together, and was quite a jovial affair, apart from the standard of food which hadn't gone up at all, myself and Ken took a wander up the road to see what was what. Walking up the so called main street there wasn't a lot to rave about and the only real shop was the Hudson Bay Trading Post which sold just about everything imaginable, rather like a ship's chandlers for landlubbers. I bought a couple of souvenirs just to prove I had actually been here and then we went for a coffee in the only coffee bar in town. As we roamed around we came across an old cinema which was called, very aptly, "The Igloo", which was showing a film that evening which wasn't too many years out of date, so we decided to return that evening for an evening's entertainment. The only very large building in town was the Canadian Army Camp which I believe had been there many years and, we found out, that we were allowed to use the NAAFI facilities which we took advantage of and were made very welcome. I suppose that stuck up there it made a nice change for them to talk to some outsiders and stopped them going mad with each other's company. The thing that surprised me as we walked back to the ship was how warm it was and we were even plagued by hungry mosquitoes which left us itching all over, but I was sure that the life of a mosquito here wasn't a long one.

The next morning dockers started coming aboard and we started to open our hatches up to start loading our cargo of grain. It would take about two days to load and I was to work with the chippy to make sure that the shifting boards were okay. When you load a cargo of grain you have to erect shifting boards which stops the loose grain from moving and causing the ship to list and possibly turn over. They are made out of timber and are the shape of a lift shaft going down into the hold and this stops the cargo moving. The other way it can be done is to fill sacks with grain and lay them on top of the loose cargo and I have had this system used when bringing grain from South America. But this time it was shifting boards. By the end of the first day we were starting to go lower in the water as the holds were slowly filling and the fine grain dust was getting everywhere. That evening, after dinner, I went with Ken up to the army base again and had a pleasant time and found the Canadians a good crowd and very hospitable and as we staggered back to the ship we kept a beady eye open for any hungry polar bears and, we were informed, wolves!

The following morning we started to get ready for sea and as the holds were not filled up I asked about this and was told we were going to St. Johns, Newfoundland to top up and take on bunkers. We covered the hatches and lowered the derricks and secured all down. As we were now nearly down to our plimsoll line the whole ship sat down in the water and the distance to me from the sea to the deck didn't seem far at all! We sailed at 12.00 and as the last rope was cast off from the shore the longshore man shouted good luck to us and told us we were the last ship out this year. I assumed that Churchill was now closed. The Chief Officer told me that I was still on 4-8 until St. Johns then I could go on day work, of which I was very pleased. As I went on watch the following morning at 04.00 I noticed that the ship was slowed right down, even though the weather was not too bad apart from turning very cold, and the 3rd Mate said that the Hudson had started to freeze and the Captain wanted to get to the ice field in daylight. As the sun slowly rose the sea around us was solidifying and ahead of us the whole sea had turned white as we approached the ice field very slowly. What a sight as we gently crunched our way through the pancake ice and looking astern we left a dark line in the ice as far as you could see until it froze over again. What a God forsaken place I thought and prayed that the dear old engines kept us going as I didn't fancy spending Christmas stuck in the middle of the Hudson. It took us a few hours to get clear of the flow and we then entered clear water and increased our speed to full ahead and headed for the straits and then on to St. Johns, which would take about five days. The weather was still kind to us as we came out of the straits and headed south we didn't see much only the occasional iceberg and one day we met up with one of the huge ice breaking vessels. I was told to call it up on the Aldis lamp and have a chat with it. Luckily his morse code was as slow as mine so we could understand each other. I remember once when I was 2nd Mate I called a ship up at night just for a friendly chat and this mass of flashes came back at such a speed I put the lamp away and forgot all about it. Most probably a Royal Navy vessel with a professional signaller on the end of it.

We got to St. Johns at 19.30 and started loading straight away and had to work through the night so no chance to even get ashore for a look around. As soon as our holds were full we moved over to the bunkering jetty and started to fill our hungry tanks, and when they were topped up we were off to sea again having been in St. Johns for about twelve hours in total. The weather had turned very nasty with very heavy wind and sea, pouring with rain and a nice bit of fog to cap it all. As we were well deep in the water we were a lot more stable, but the problem now was taking heavy seas over the bows and they swept down the foredeck and quite often into the alleyways, finishing up flooding our cabins. I spent plenty of time mopping up and trying to get our gear dry. But there were some plus points as I found it very thrilling to stand on the bridge and watch the ships bows go into a heavy sea, wondering if they would come up again and then see the water crashing down the deck and filter back into the sea. The sea is a wondrous thing and the power of it awesome to be treated with a great deal of respect and care.

The other thing I was learning was the comradeship and discipline in the Merchant Navy. Unless you have been in one of the services I don't think that you know the comradeship that you find in a closely knit group of men and some of the men I sailed with were really tough and some very nasty, but they would never let you down and if they gave their word on something they would never break it. The other thing was the discipline in the Merchant Navy. There was no standing to attention and saluting, but orders were given and they were carried out in a quiet way and when in a storm or in a nasty situation every one pulled together. I suppose that it was we were all in the same boat and our lives depended on each other.

I was now on day work which was a nice change from having to stand watches and get up at some unearthly hour each day. The Captain had a bee in his bonnet about the ship's appearance and I suppose he wanted to show the shipping company when we arrived back in the U.K. that he had tried to make some effort. Out came the chipping hammers, red lead, gloss and varnish and we set-to to try and make a silk purse out of a sow's ear. On one fairly flat day I had the pleasure of painting the foremast and to be hauled up to the top of the mast in a bosun's chair and worked my way down, one minute over the ships deck, the next over the sea as the ship slowly rolled and me trying to put paint on the mast, not all over me. It's funny as I didn't mind heights then, but if I stand on a chair now I get vertigo, but I suppose I was young and didn't give a damn for much. One job I had to do, I did get a pat on the back for it from the Chief Officer, and that was that one of the wire back springs had broken when we left Churchill and I had to splice it. Anyone who had spliced wire knows that it isn't an easy job, but I got it done even though it was heavy wire and a bitch to do.

Each Sunday we had the Captain's inspection when he and the Chief Officer toured the ship to make sure all was okay and checked all the cabins to see if all was in order and there wasn't any women smuggled aboard. He usually staggered round with his ever present smell of Scotch about him, then he, the Chief Officer and the Chief Engineer got down to some serious drinking whilst discussing any problems that might have appeared on their rounds. We also had a fire drill which was a bit of a failure as when we ran out the fire hoses they had so many holes in them that not much water reached the nozzle. I had to check the extinguishers and they seemed pretty low as I was informed that the C.T.C. ones got abused as the contents of them were very good for cleaning spots and marks off suits and uniforms so they had

30

to be checked regularly, especially after leaving port and people had done a spot of dry cleaning before going ashore!

The jobs were very varied. The days when the weather permitted us to work outside we did work like scrapping down the woodwork in the front of the bridge and giving it a coat of varnish or giving the funnel a paint which looked quite nice for about five minutes until the engineers decided to blow the boilers which covered the wet paint in black smuts and sent the Chief Officer off his rocker. On wet days jobs like making canvas covers for the fire extinguishers, or painting some of the cabins in any colour as long as it was white. I worked alongside the crew on a lot of the jobs and they tolerated me - just. Some of the stories they came up with were beyond belief and also what they had done but as I have said, most of them had bad discharges from other ships. They all had one aim in common and that was at the end of the trip to get off as quickly as possible.

And so we plodded east and after about ten days and a few more engine failures we got our orders to make for Liverpool to discharge the cargo and then the ship was having a few days in dry dock for a survey to make sure that she was still sea worthy and could float. We picked the pilot up at the bar and made our way up the Mersey to our berth. It was a very nice feeling to ring up on the telegraph "finished with engines" when we were safely alongside with our ropes and springs to the shore. The Captain and the pilot charged off the bridge to the Captain's cabin to have a few Scotches to celebrate that we had made it without sinking or destroying anything. As I tidied up the bridge I thought, the end of my first trip and what a lot I had learnt and that I had grown up very quickly. But all that mattered at that period of time was that tomorrow I was going on leave!

Chapter 3

Dirty Cargo

What a joy it was to be back home, to eat decent food, drink decent drinks, and all without the taste of grease and the faint hint of oil. What a joy it was to sleep in a bed without the sheets feeling damp and salty and best of all was that everything stayed still without rolling or pitching all over the place. I know that I moaned about the ship, food and bad weather and high seas and said to my friends what a rotten way to make a living, but when they all had to get to their work on a Monday morning at 9 o'clock and sat in their mundane offices until Friday, I thought, maybe my way was better and at least I didn't know what was round the corner, or over the next wave. I supposed that I showed off to my friends, talking about icebergs, polar bears and horrendous seas, but they tolerated me and at least it was a good talking point with the girls! I'm not too sure how my parents took it all when I explained about the shipping company and the state of the ship, as I think that they thought I would return after my first trip as an officer and a gentleman. As I seemed to bring a different girl home each night, they were very good and must have realised that it was only a short leave and the household would soon return to normal once I departed back to sea.

And it was to be. After eight days the dreaded telegram arrived telling me to return to my beloved ship in Liverpool and so that was the end of my few days of sanity and it was back to the joys of the mad cooks concoctions and the odd way of life I had chosen. As I said goodbye to my parents and friends and sat on the train from Canterbury up to London I prayed to God that this trip would be to somewhere warm and not back to the frozen wastes, but thinking on I realised that the Hudson would now be frozen over so that trip was out. I wondered what cargo we could bring back from the south pole area! When I arrived in Liverpool I found out that the ship was still in dry dock and that the Chief Officer had sent me a second telegram telling me to stay at home for a few more days. Great news! I left the shipping office in not too good a mood and got a taxi to take me down to the dry dock and seek out the old tub. The taxi found the ship and as I walked from the gangway on to the ship I peered down and thought, that's a long way to the bottom, and the ship sitting like that without any water round her and propped up with large timbers so she wouldn't fall over, reminded me of a stranded whale.

I reported to the 1st Mate after I had dumped my travelling bag in my cabin and he was most surprised, and upset that I hadn't received his second telegram to keep me on leave for another week. He wasn't as upset as I was! He told me that we would be in dry dock for about another seven days and that the only other people on board were the Chief Engineer, chief steward and the bosun, and the rest of the crew had all signed off vowing never to sail under this company's colours again, only if press ganged. The rest of the officers were on leave and would rejoin when we were ready to load and that it would be the same Captain as last trip. I wondered what terrible thing he had done to deserve this vessel and was he doomed to go round and round the world in this rust bucket forever!

Staying on board a ship in dry dock is an odd sensation and the whole of the ship felt dead as most of the engine machinery was out of action apart from possibly one generator and the rest of the power came from cables from the shore. During the day chaos ruled with dockers all over the place welding here, repairing there with cables and wires all over the place and to me total confusion, but at 5pm when they all did a runner down the gangways and headed for their nice cosy homes, silence fell and it was quite an eerie feeling. Once during smoko I climbed down to the bottom of the dock and peered up at our great hull and ships sides, I also went to the stern to take a closer look at the propeller that pushed us through the waters at such a fantastic speed, and prayed that it stayed on. It was quite awesome to see how much of the ship was under the water line and standing down there she seemed gigantic, and also very rusty. There wasn't much work for me to do, but the 1st Mate found me some jobs each day and after dinner in the evening, which consisted of me, Chief Engineer and Chief Officer trying to force down what the steward had managed to dish up in these adverse conditions, I used to go up the road to a cinema to try and get warm for a few hours. Dry dock isn't my favourite place on earth.

After about seven unpleasant days we moved out of the dock and round to our loading berth. As we only had a skeleton crew on board I was put in charge of the stern during this operation and felt very important with my two gangers to give a hand, but I think I got in the way more than I actually helped. It was nice to watch the water slowly rise in the dock and the great shoring timbers pulled away as we floated once more and the tugs towed us out of the dock and round to our new berth. I had now learnt that we would be taking cars out to the southern states of America and then picking up a bulk cargo for our return trip. That night I slept well with the thought of going to America and some nice warm weather to help us on our way with an easy cargo to bring back. Once again I was to be proved wrong.

The next day the crew started coming on board and they didn't seem much of an improvement on the last lot, except these all came from Liverpool, most with DRs or double DRs (bad reports from other ships). The officers arrived, some from the last trip, some new ones, and the Captain arrived back pretty well legless, as I supposed that he was so pleased to see his lovely ship once again! A new senior cadet called John joined as Ken was signed off sick and I wondered if he had a nervous breakdown or paid the doctor to give him a sick note to miss sailing. The general feeling of joining or returning to the ship seemed to be of doom and despondency and the atmosphere in the saloon that night over dinner wasn't one of joy and happiness. Our cargo had started to be loaded and the new cars were hoisted off the dockside and lowered into our hatches by the ships derricks and lovely old steam winches. I only saw one mishap, one of the winches started slipping as one of the cars were high in the air and it finished up over the ships rails after plunging at a great speed on to them. What a waste of a brand new car.

The cars were lowered on to the deck of the hold then driven by a docker or a crew member to within inches of each other and secured by a rope round the wheels with a length of timber in it, then twisted until taut so they wouldn't move in bad weather. Each day of the trip all the cars had to be checked to make sure they were secure and it was very pleasant to sit in them, start the engine and dream. All the cars had a brand new tool kit in them when they arrived on board, but when they got to the States many hadn't, but the crew and dockers had. When the lower decks were filled we put the hatch covers on and then started on the tween decks and at the same time the ships stores and bond were being hoisted aboard and by 17.00 hours we had a full cargo and were battened down and ready to sail at midnight. When the pilot came aboard the Chief Officer told me to take the wheel for leaving harbour, so my steering must have improved somewhat. We left Liverpool and headed back down the Mersey and once the pilot was off the ship and we were in clear waters I was relieved on the wheel and told to get some shut eye as I had been on the go for eighteen hours and by then was pretty worn out. When I got shaken at breakfast time I noticed that the ship was only going slow ahead and the 3rd told me that one of the boilers was damaged and it would take a couple of hours for the engineers to do repairs. So much for dry dock!

I was put back on the 4-8 watch so back to early mornings, back to studying and also after a couple of days back to bad weather. Life got back into routine, with a couple of diversions to break the monotony such as one day we were joined by a school of porpoises and it was great as they played and jumped around the bows with a big grin on their faces and they banged themselves against the stem of the ship, some say to knock parasites off them, but if this is true I don't know. It was nice to have them as company for a couple of hours then off they sped at a great rate of knots to God knows where. Another diversion was when the weather got so rough the Captain had to stop her so that she didn't break herself up. That day the distance covered in twenty four hours by us was about 10 miles, backwards. As the weather moderated the following day the radio officer came to the bridge and informed the Captain that he had heard a German grain ship in distress not too far away from us. The 2nd Mate laid a course off to intercept the stricken ship and we altered our course towards it, but after a few hours no more was heard from it so we came back round to our correct course. I wonder what happened to it?

After about a week out from the U.K. the weather started to take a turn for the better and it was nice not to be forever mopping up the cabin and my clothes in my lockers started to dry out. The Mate got us all out on deck with the chipping hammers and paint and once again tried to tart her up again and get rid of some of the rust. At least it was pleasant to work in the sunshine just with a pair of shorts and a tee shirt on instead of souwester's and wellingtons.

Another diversion after seventeen days and this turned out to be very nice in an odd sort of way. I was doing my trig at the wheel on a beautiful day with a flat sea, the 3rd Mate was half asleep hanging over the open bridge windows and the Captain was in the chart room doing some paperwork, when the cook appeared on the bridge wing and asked to see the old man as it was of great importance to the ship. The Captain came out of the chart room and the cook informed him that within twenty four hours he wouldn't be able to do any more cooking as he was going to run out of oil for the galley stove! The Captain went spare! The cook said it wasn't his fault and there was a real ding dong of a row with the cook blaming the ship for being so slow and kept breaking down, and the Captain calling the cook everything under the sun. Eventually the cook stormed off the bridge saying that if the Captain didn't want a mutiny he had better do something about it. As luck would have it our course for the southern States wasn't too far off Bermuda and the old man got the 2nd Mate to lay a course off to head us for that lovely island, which wasn't too many miles away. This was the sort of diversion I liked especially if I had a chance to get ashore and have a look around! The Captain left the bridge in a fine rage and locked himself in his cabin for a few hours with a couple of bottles of Scotch to calm his frayed nerves.

After about eighteen hours steaming we approached Hamilton, the capital of Bermuda, and got tied up alongside the jetty and joy of joys we had to stay twenty four hours to get the galley oil and then top up our own bunkers. So that meant a look around in the afternoon then ashore in the evening for a local meal and a few drinks. The cook wasn't such a bad man after all, I thought, even though he couldn't cook. That was a very pleasant day and as we hadn't any work to do apart from John, poor chap who was told to do gangway watch, and a couple of the engineers who had to see to the oil coming aboard, most of the officers and crew opted for a few hours ashore. I went up to town with the 3rd Mate and he quickly introduced me to rum and coke, of which I took to like a duck to water. In one of the bars we got talking to one of the friendly barmen who told us a bit about Bermuda and I was surprised to learn that there was 360 islands, of which only 20 were inhabited, and that the one we were on was called Long Island. The population was about 56,000 and that there was no surface water on the island, hence I thought everyone drank rum and coke. Heaven! He said that both the British and Americans had large Air Force and Naval bases here and that it was one of the Americans favourite holiday spots as well as being an American tax haven. It was called millionaires paradise and we soon found that out by the cost of things and our small amount of shore money soon started to disappear. After a few more drinks in different bars we had a look at the price of a meal and decided it was beyond our reach so invested the rest of our money in some more rums and staggered quite happily back to the ship to eat on board. I mean to say, who would want to eat crayfish when we could have corned beef fritters! But it had been nice to stretch our legs and see how the other half lived.

We sailed the following day with lots of hangovers and quite a few of the crew had black eyes and scars from the discussion they had with the U.S. Navy, but we hadn't lost any crew member which must have been a plus point. We headed west once more towards southern Carolina which was only about 700 miles away so at our 9 knots it was about three days steaming. The weather was beautiful and the sea a lovely blue and when you looked astern of the ship you could see the white wake of the ship disappear into the far yonder and at night the same thing. All on board seemed happy and even the old man seemed in a cheerful mood and had changed into his off white uniform. After three and a half days the steering gear jammed for a few hours, we approached Charleston and after berthing the dockers came on board and unloading started and as we were only going to land half our cargo we would only be in port for about eight hours before going down the coast to unload the rest at Jacksonville, Florida. No shore leave, but after Bermuda this industrial town did look very drab and I think its main claim to fame was that it was here that the American Civil War started. I walked up to a local cafe with the 2nd Engineer at lunchtime, just to get the feel of the American way of life, but that was as far as we went and at about 17.00 we had the pilot on board and we were heading out to sea once more. From Charleston to Jacksonville was only 200 miles, or a days sailing, so the ropes didn't have to be stowed away and as the weather was so fine some of the hatches were only half covered ready to discharge the rest of the cars. At least we would arrive in the evening so we could get a run ashore, but this wasn't to be for as soon as we arrived we started unloading and we were only in for just over eight hours. As we sailed down the St. Johns river on which Jacksonville stands, once again it didn't look too inviting and as far as I could find out from one of the dockers it was famous for shipbuilding, chemicals, lumber, printing and cigars and he said tourism, which I couldn't see but maybe it had an attractive side somewhere.

As we cleared the St. Johns river I asked John what our next port of call was as we were stowing the mooring ropes away and he said "Bloody Port Sulphur" and wouldn't say much else. Funny name for a port I mused and when I approached the 2nd Mate about it he said that it was up the Mississippi and the cargo was bulk sulphur. Logical cargo for the port name I thought. The weather was still superb, but there was an atmosphere on the ship which wasn't good as the crew had found out what the cargo was to be and there was much moaning and mumbling. I was told that sulphur was not a very pleasant cargo and that it got everywhere and burnt like hell and that our destination with it was Italy, which was quite a long haul. We headed nearly due south making for the Florida straits which was about 300 miles passing the Bahamas to port then round the bottom of Florida and Key West then into the Gulf of Mexico and another 600 miles to the Mississippi delta. We plodded along at our 9 knots, high out of the water as we were a light ship and after about five days we entered the mouth of the great Mississippi and picked up our pilot. The thing that struck me was how flat the country was and high up on our bridge we could see for miles. As we tied up at our berth at Sulphur I looked down on the flat town and the ship seemed to tower over it. We weren't going to start to load until the next day so John and I walked up to the small town to have a look around and then sample the local beer. In one of the bars we met the local sheriff with a gun on his hip, ten gallon on his head and a broad Louisiana drawl. He was very friendly and after a couple of drinks with him he asked us if we would like to see a real American jail. We jumped into his very large police car and after charging down the high street we arrived at his place of work and he started to show us the jail. It was very modern with a lot of electronic equipment of which he was proud of and after a cup of coffee he asked me if I had ever been behind bars and I said of course not, unsure of what he was getting at. He took us down to the jail block of which there was three cells all of which had a prisoner in and when he asked one of them if he minded if I could join him for a few minutes, just to get the feel of it, this big black man said he didn't mind at all. The sheriff pressed a button and whoosh the bars slid open, I stepped in and whoosh the bars closed behind me. I had a nice chat to my fellow prisoner for about five minutes, he asking me about England and me asking him all about America, and when I was released from my cell we shook hands and wished each other well. Upstairs over another cup of coffee I said what a polite man the prisoner was and what was he in prison for. The sheriff said he was in for murder and that the next day he was being moved to a larger prison and was expecting to go on to

Death Row! Charming I thought. We bade goodbye to our friendly sheriff and decided to return to one of the bars in town to sample the delights of the American steak over a couple more beers before returning to the ship. Before turning in that night I decided to look in the dictionary the definition of sulphur and it stated 'Pale yellow element occurring in crystal, burns with a blue flame and has a stifling smell, makes matches, gunpowder, vulcanite and sulphuric acid.' I had wondered what the pungent smell was that hung over the town and thought this wasn't the place to live or settle down in. I switched my bunk light off and didn't look forward to the next day.

After breakfast we uncovered the hatches and started loading. The sulphur was carried up from the dock by large conveyor belts then shot into our holds and soon the whole ship was covered in a blanket of yellow. We were given gauze nose protectors, but this didn't help too much and soon our eyes were streaming and getting sore and burnt. This filthy stuff got every-where, in the cabins, in our clothes, in the food, everywhere. Looking at the ships hand rails you could see the fire running along them and the whole ship seemed to glow and the stink was appalling. We loaded all day and most of the night and I eventually managed to get three hours sleep before having to get the hatches covered and make the ship ready for sea. We let the ropes go at 09.30 and as we slipped away from the jetty all on board breathed a sigh of relief as we moved down the Mississippi towards the open sea and fresh air and it wasn't very often that everyone was pleased to leave a port, but in this instance this was the case. Once the hatches were all secure and the locking bars on, out came the hose pipes to try and get rid of some of the filth and the ship got a really good washing down, but it didn't help in the accommodation where everything was covered by a thin coating of yellow. It would take weeks to get rid of it and the smell lingered for ages and of course as soon as we thought that it had all cleared we then had the pleasure of discharging the damn stuff and we would be back in the same boat again.

So eastward we tramped with a pretty disgruntled crew and lots of moans and groans and not a good feeling aboard. The two queer stewards were very upset as they said that their best dresses were ruined and they hadn't got a thing to wear in Italy. Funny lot. Some of the seamen made life very unpleasant for one of the crew and kept picking on him. He was on my watch and was a very quiet nice man called Pierre and came from Malta and was about 45. One day he had enough of it and said to the biggest seaman who was the ring leader to sort it all out on No. 4 hatch with a fight. One minute later the seaman was in a pile on the top of the hatch, then Pierre asked for another one to have a go with the same result. After a couple more of them had a go at Pierre he suggested that they sat down and had a chat about it, and lo and behold they agreed and after that they left him alone. He told me later that he had spent some time in the Foreign Legion and had learnt how to take care of himself there. Life got back into routine and once again I was on the 4-8 watch so it was up with the larks each day. Back to studying, chipping, painting etc. It was quite a long haul to Savona in Italy and I worked it out to be about 6,000 miles so at 10 knots, God willing, it would take about twenty five days so we had to call in the Bahamas to pick up oil and water, but we only stayed a few hours so no shore leave. The old man stayed on the bottle and suddenly decided he would make a good teacher so for three days on the trot he gave us cadets an hours tuition but after that he got bored with it so that idea went out of the porthole. Christmas Day 1958 came and went without much fun and joy, but the cook at least tried to give us a decent meal under adverse conditions.

As we headed north the weather got worse, but as the old ship put her bows into the great seas taking great greenbacks over the stem and the water running over the forward hatches, down the alleyways and quite often into our cabins, at least she was having a good wash down. We passed through the straits of Gibraltar and into the Mediterranean with about 1,000 miles to go and as we passed the Balearic isles and headed up to Savona we weren't looking forward to discharging our terrible cargo and the whole ship once more being covered in yellow. As we approached Savona, which is the port next to Genoa, I was doing my turn at the wheel and I asked the Captain what the port was like and he explained that it was an industrial town with a population of about 75,000 and that its main industry was iron, glass, tin plate and shipbuilding and that it exported tomatoes and preserved fruit. Now that would be a nice cargo I though, a ship load of preserved fruit. We picked up our pilot and he navigated us in with a lot of arm waving and italian gestures to our berth, which seemed to be in the middle of the town. This was to be a provisional berth just for the night and tomorrow we would move round to our unloading jetty. We got our bow lines ashore and then made fast to a stern buoy so the only way we could get ashore was by a gangway from our bows to the dock, this causing me a problem later on. As we weren't going to start discharging until tomorrow apart from a skeleton crew the rest of us made for the shore once we had been cleared by customs and immigration.

We lost a lot of the crew that night! One fell into an open sewer and contracted some horrible disease, two broke their ankles on bumper cars at the local fairground after having a skinful of local hooch and some just didn't come back and jumped ship. I went ashore with a couple of junior officers and we got stuck into the local vermouth which was pretty evil. At about 2am we had had enough and staggered back to the ship only to find that the gangplank was missing. It was there when we went ashore, now it was gone. "Don't worry", I slurred. "I will climb up the ropes and get someone to help me launch the lifeboat or something." We all thought that this was a good idea and as I was young, fit and very drunk and it didn't seem too far to climb, I set off up the rope. It was a long way and when I got to the top and tried to swing myself over I couldn't. Knackered! "Can't do it" I yelled and I let go and fell into the filthy waters of Savona harbour. By now lights were coming on aboard the ship as we were making a lot of din and I looked up and saw the Chief Engineer stagger out of his cabin and peer down at me. For some unknown reason he was wearing his best uniform and his best cap and had definitely been on the booze with some vengeance. "Don't worry Biddick" he slurred down at me, "I will save you" and without any more ado he leapt over the rails and surfaced in the water next to me and for some unknown reason he still had his nice new cap on his head. "I can swim", I said to him. "Oh shit!" he replied, and we both made our way back to the quay. Next morning over a very quiet breakfast as everyone was nursing giant hangovers, the Captain said to the Chief Engineer, "I saw what happened last night Chief and I don't know whether to put you on a charge or put you forward for a medal." We continued our breakfast in silence.

What remaining crew members we had gave us a hand to move the ship round to the unloading berth and once again we got covered in that terrible yellow stuff and as the Italians didn't seem to work half the pace the Americans did it took us just on a week to clear our holds. In the meantime, the shipping company had to fly out replacement crew to replace the "Ones that got away" and they didn't seem much better as they arrived a day late and pretty well legless when they got on board. From Savona the ship was going into dry dock again as the boiler was still giving the engineers a problem, but a least the dry docking was to be in London. So with an empty ship we left Italy and headed back across the Mediterranean towards the straits of Gibraltar and at least this time we passed through in daylight and we got a good view of the rock. During the twelve days it would take us to get to London we had the unenviable job of cleaning the holds and bilges and as we were a light ship it was very unpleasant to be stuck down the holds in the middle of the Bay of Biscay in a force 9 with the ship rolling all over the place like a pig. The replacement crew were not impressed and couldn't wait to sign off, even though they would have only been on this cruise ship for a few days. We rounded Ushant and started to tramp our way up the English Channel and all of a sudden everyone's spirits rose and life didn't seem too bad after all. It was nice to see glimpses of England on the port hand side and we all got talking about leave and what we would do and all hoped to get a transfer to another one of the ships in the company, a more modern one than this. We rounded the north foreland and started making for the Thames Estuary and the end was in sight. Once we had entered the dry dock and the ship was once again shored up the officers and the crew started to leave, leaving just a few members on board. After nearly four and a half months aboard on this trip it was quite enough for anyone and as I walked down the gangway I thought how nice to have a few days of sanity before the next trip into the unknown.

Chapter 4

West Africa

Six days, then the telegram. That didn't seem a very long leave or very fair, but mine was not to reason why and my orders were to join the old ship once more, not in London, but a place called Burntisland up on the Firth of Forth, just under the Forth bridge. The ship had undergone a quick dry dock and had been moved up there to start loading general cargo for a place called Takoradi in West Africa. For the next five months I would be on this run and at least the cargo was a darn sight better than the last lot. So once more I said goodbye to my friends and my parents, promising them that I would bring them back a parrot from Africa even though they insisted I shouldn't bother and not too keen on the idea, and got a train from Canterbury to London then boarded the Queen of Scots express for Edinburgh. At Edinburgh I changed to the slow local service that took me on to Burntisland which had to cross the Forth bridge and on that trip and each other one I made over the bridge I always thought of one of my favourite books, John Buchan's "The 39 Steps". Funny how the brain works! At Burntisland I got off the train and walked down to the small docks and could see that about three smallish ships was all that this little port could take and that you had to lock in and out. I came to love this little community and a couple of times that we returned from Africa the Captain asked if I would like a few days leave I asked if I could stay aboard instead. The population was only about 6,000 and at night the pubs would lock you in, not throw you out. I assumed that the old man must have thought that he was in seventh heaven with all that Scotch around and bigger tots. The nearest decent size town was Kirkaldy, a few miles along, and I spent many happy hours there improving Scottish/English relationships with the local girls.

Once aboard and settled in again, I found that most of the officers from the last trip had been relieved and were on leave or had joined other ships of the company. The new lot seemed to be a good bunch as I got to know them and I also had a new cadet join me in my cabin who was in his last year of his cadetship and for the next few trips got down to some hard studying before he had to go to college and this encouraged me to do the same. All of the last trips crew had not returned, believe it or not, and most of the new lot were Scottish, many from the islands, and I found them a nice crowd and very good seamen who also liked their drink. I remember once leaving Takoradi one night with the old man drunk out of his brains, the helmsman drunk as a skunk and the pilot didn't know whether he was coming or going after a session with the old man. How we survived some of these escapades I will never know. But as the old man was a Scot like the rest of the crew it was a happy ship and even the cooking had taken a turn for the better, on Good Friday the cook surprised the whole ship by producing some form of hot cross buns.

With our cargo of general goods, this ranging from anything you cared to mention, we bade a fond farewell to bonny Scotland and the ship passed out of the small lock and into the Firth of Forth, then down the eastern coast of Britain before turning in the Channel. I always got a bit homesick as we passed Dover as my home was only about 20 miles away and I thought what the hell am I doing out here. Down the Channel we plodded, trying to miss the ferries crossing our bows, then round Ushant, across Biscay once more heading south. Once near the Canary Isles the weather started to warm up and we changed into our whites for wearing on the bridge and when eating in the saloon, but on deck I just used to wear a pair of working shorts.

Our first port of call after about fourteen days was Dakor, the capital of Senegal, where we used to pick up oil and water so we only stayed a few hours at the most. That was enough. Once we had got the ropes ashore and the ship lay still, the heat hit you like a blast furnace and took your breath away and as we were on the oil jetty, which was quite a way from the town, I never even had a chance to look around, even had I wished to. It was very nice to cast off and get under a bit of breeze to cool us off. From Dakor to Takoradi was about 1,500 miles so about six days steaming, without breakdowns, so it was back to the old routine of on watch, studying, chipping, painting, greasing etc etc. At least on the first trip we actually had a passenger. It was all a mystery. He was a chap of eighteen and was going out to West Africa. For why, we never found out. For why this old ship we didn't know. The only thing that we thought that it must have been a very cheap fare and that he was some form of masochist. Still, it gave us something to talk about and some of the theories were mind boggling.

We travelled down the coast of Africa passing Sierra Leone and Liberia before turning nearly due east along the latitude of 3° north which meant we were about 300 miles north of the equator, and it felt like it. Our cabins were boiling and the so called blower system just circulated the hot air and we stayed hot and sticky. The best place to be was on the bridge and at least you could get some form of cool air either on the bridge wing as lookout or on the wheel with the breeze blowing through the open bridge windows. The sea was like a mirror as our course just clipped the doldrums and every now and then you could see a fin cruise past, also you could see a flying fish take off, fly for a while then plop back into the ocean. At night they seemed to be attracted to the ships lights and if you left your porthole open they actually flew into the cabin. We found a few of them on the ships deck and they are very colourful, but thank

God, the cook never gave them to us for our evening meal. As we approached Cape Three Points, which is close to Takoradi, the radio officer gave the Captain a message saying that we would have to go to the anchorage for two days as our berth wasn't clear. Once we had dropped our hook the old man called the bosun and told him this was a good chance to paint the ships sides so for the next couple of days we roasted sitting on stages slapping paint on the sides. We didn't get too close to the water as we remembered those fins cruising around a few days ago.

The pilot came out to us at last and we hauled up our anchor and headed into port and were informed that we would be there at least three days discharging and then loading. Safely alongside I got the first feeling of Africa which was very hot, dusty and not a very pleasant smell about the place, and by the time the dockers knocked off in the evening we well deserved a cool shower, sort of cool, and then a pre dinner beer. Over dinner that night the Captain, who had been on the booze during the afternoon to quench his thirst, said to me that if I went ashore that night I was to go with the 2nd and 3rd Mate as he didn't want me to get into any trouble. He mumbled on about the terrible responsibility it was looking after the youngsters aboard and as the 2nd told him that he would look after my welfare I saw him give the 3rd Mate a wink. I was told to be ready to go ashore at 21.00 hours so I went back to my cabin after dinner and got changed into a pair of slacks and a freshly ironed shirt and at the duly appointed hour I made my way along to the 3rd's cabin and found him and the 2nd well and truly stuck into a case of beer. When a few more beers had been sunk we went down the gangway and made our way up town, passing some very pleasant open sewers on the way. Having gone through the main part of town we finished up in a seedy bar in the back streets and my two companions seem to have been here before as they got a warm welcome. It was a very dimly lit bar and I couldn't understand why there seemed to be a lot of young ladies sitting on stools by themselves and there was a heavy smell of cheap perfume when the girls walked past to dance on the small dance floor to the sound of slow music. One of these big black beauties kept on looking and smiling at me and after about an hour and some considerable beers later she looked quite pretty. She called the 2nd Mate over and whispered in his ear and he nodded and she gave a giggle and came over to me and draped herself all over me and tried to eat me. I found out later that she had asked him if the young lad, me, was a virgin and he had said yes! After trying to suffocate me with her ample breasts she took my hand and led me out of the bar and down a couple of back streets and we finished up on the outskirts of the jungle and entered a mud hut. She stripped off in double time and showed me her very black body then started to strip me and we finished up on the hut floor on a form of matting where she took advantage of my young body and had her wicked way with me. About an hour later and pounds of sweat off me I reached for my trousers and remembered that the chief steward had issued us with anti V.D. kits so after applying three tubes of penicillin to my thing I thought that no known germs could have survived that onslaught considering that one was ample. Eat your heart out Domestos! I returned to the bar, leaving my tutor lying there with a happy smile on her face, and met up again with my ship mates who by then were almost legless and we made our way back to the ship to climb into our welcoming bunks. Over breakfast the Captain asked me if the two mates had kept me out of trouble and I said yes, feeling myself going as red as a beetroot.

Today was Sunday so no unloading and the 3rd took me up to a swimming club which was for the local British residences and it was all very civilised with a pleasant bar and restaurant in which we had a very tasty lunch and met some of the locals who made us more than welcome and then invited us back to one of their houses for afternoon tea and cakes and by about 6 o'clock we bade them farewell and made our way back to the ship as we both were suffering from last nights exploits. The next day we finished unloading and then started to load our cargo of palm oil, cocoa and gigantic logs which mostly went as deck cargo as they were too big to go down the holds and we had to secure them with chains over them and then fasten to the deck. They were hard wood and I'm not sure if they were mahogany or teak the only thing I do know was that they were some fair size. As the loading proceeded and the plimsoll line got closer to the water line, I, being a good son, remembered that I had said I would take my parents a parrot home, to make them very happy people! By now a few African greys had appeared on board and the peace of the evening was shattered by the mad shriekings of these birds. Each day a man came on to the ship selling them so I selected one and he told me it was a good choice as it was a nice quiet, friendly bird who would make a good pet. From the time I had paid the man and he had gone down the gangway at a gallop with my money in his hand to the time I sold it there was no love lost between us at all and his one aim in life was to maim me. I called him Tug and by the time I got back to the U.K. I was lucky to have any fingers left and he was lucky I hadn't stretched his neck. One day on the trip back I took him out on to the hatch as I had been told that his wings had been clipped so he couldn't fly. Wrong again, as I saw him take off and fly up to the cross trees of the foremast and I must admit as he sat there looking down at me I thought, jump you bastard and head for your homeland but no, he half flew, half fell heading back to me and upon landing had a good go at me. I eventually got him back to Canterbury and as I could see that my parents weren't too impressed with my gift, as they couldn't get near it, the next day I took it down to the local pet shop and got £25 for it. A year or so later I found out that the pet shop owner had sold it to one of the local pubs and that it turned out to be a brilliant talker, but I still think that I had done the right thing and I'm sure my parents thought so!

The other wonderful gift that Takoradi gave me was malaria! We had just left the port returning back to the U.K. when I went down with it and as the chief steward was supposed to be the medical officer aboard and really didn't know anything about it at all he had to ask medical advice via the radio officer to find out what I had and the cure. Laying in my bunk sweating like mad I wondered if I had caught some nasty disease from that black girl or was it that bloody parrot that had given me something! I floated in and out of consciousness and eventually started to get better after a week or so. At least it got me off my watch duties. Another time I got a relapse was when I was a stand by crew in London and that evening I had gone up town to see a Jerry Lewis film when half way through it I felt bad and left the cinema. Walking along the road I suddenly just passed out and when I came round I looked up and saw a big London bobby peering down at me saying "Well laddie and what have we been drinking?" I managed to get out that I was having a bout of malaria and was then whisked away to Charing Cross hospital where I was kept for about a week. They were brilliant there and when I was feeling better one of the nurses made me feel most welcome and it always seems the case that nurses and seamen seem to have a bond and always get on with each other. One of the times I got malaria was the closest I've come to death and was a weird sensation. I was on a ship as 2nd Mate and we were just leaving a port in Norway bringing back a cargo of paper pulp to London. As 2nd Mate I was in charge of the casting off operation at the stern of the ship when I just passed out and fell into the snow on the deck. I was carried to the chief steward's cabin by two seamen and laid on his bunk. All I remember was that I was floating around the top of the cabin looking down and saw myself laying on the bunk with the steward taking my temperature saying "Christ his temperature is 105 so he should be dead!" AS it was freezing outside he didn't even think about malaria so had no idea what was wrong with me. I eventually floated down and re-entered my body, but wasn't a lot of help as I was delirious and was gibbering. I felt the ships prop dig into the water and she headed full speed for England and eventually I was put ashore at Gravesend, in the isolation hospital. I stayed there for about a week then was allowed home for a few days home rest. At least I got Christmas at home that year, but I can think of nicer ways to get some leave. People ask me if malaria hurts and I can't say that it hurts, but you just seem to float from the real world to the unreal world feeling one moment that you are burning up and the next that you have been laid in ice. Thanks Takoradi!!!

I was always pretty glad when the holds were full and we headed out to sea once more, but it had shown me an insight to that part of the world and what rural Africa was all about, the smells and atmosphere. Once clear of the port it was back to the old routine and a return trip of about twenty one days without stopping at Dakor for bunkers. But it's odd the sea and you never know from one day to the next what's going to happen, like the day we were quietly steaming along and the next moment the ship was covered with moth type things, sort of locusts and a variety of different insects. We were miles from land so where they came from and after a few hours most of them flew off to heaven knows where. All very strange. Just like the Captain on his Sunday rounds. One Sunday he would come round and everything was fine and he seemed quite sane, the next he would appear with white gloves, testing for dust and muck in corners and I think on those days he thought that he was a Captain of a destroyer or something. And so we headed back towards the Canary Islands and by then the weather was changing and it started to cool down a bit so off with the whites and back into our blue uniforms. One of the mornings I got a real telling off for being late on watch as I had forgot to alter my wristwatch. Each day the clocks on board the ship had to be changed by some many minutes per day according to how far the ship had moved along a longitudinal line, just like flying to Spain or Greece on holiday but that is done in one go, but on ship it is done in minutes. I didn't forget again. As I've said before it's always nice to turn into the Channel and start heading in the Dover direction as you realise the end is nearly in sight. On one trip we were ordered to go into Plymouth to discharge some of our cargo and myself and the other cadet managed to get ashore to stretch our legs and we finished up on the Hoe which was very pleasant. As we were walking along we were passing a Royal Navy recruiting caravan when this Chief Petty Officer leapt out on us and led us inside and commenced to tell us the joys of joining the Royal Navy and that a fine pair of lads like us would do well. After about an hour and a half of him going on about it and he started to get the signing papers out we eventually told him that it was too late and that we were cadets in the Merchant service. He wasn't too pleased about that and told us to "Sod off and don't waste my time." Charming I thought. Another time we crossed the R.N. was one day when we were steaming up the Channel minding our own business and it was quite foggy so I was on the bridge wing as look out. The 2nd Mate was having a chat with me when we heard this sort of whistle sound seeming to pass just over the mast. After this happened a couple of times the 2nd called the old man up to the bridge and he eventually got the wireless officer to send out a message to the mainland to try and find out what was going on. The message came back very fast that we were in the middle of a Royal Navy firing practice and that sound was the noises of shells passing over and around us! We moved out of that area pretty quick.

So we returned to our little haven in Scotland. As I pointed out before sometimes I went home on leave, sometimes I stayed up north and enjoyed the hospitality of the Scots. Surprisingly we kept most of the same crew whilst we were on that run and as I have already said, it was a happy ship. At last I was told to pack my bags and have the leave due to me which was about three weeks and I didn't know if I was to return to the same ship or if the ship was coming off that run and head for some other part of the world. That was up to the God's at the shipping office, but for the time being it was leave for me and once more a bit of sanity.

Chapter 5

Up the Plate

Heaven! I had been at home just about three weeks when the company sent me a telegram to join my ship in Rotterdam. Not the old one that I had just left, but one that was only two years old. 5,471 gross tons and a possible speed of 12 knots, of which I would believe when we were doing it. But this was a step in the right direction. The only thing that I didn't know was that the next couple of trips on her would keep me out of the U.K. for eight months and no leave in between.

The next day I travelled up to the shipping agents office in London to pick up my flight tickets and made my way to the airport for my night flight to Rotterdam. I was quite excited as I hadn't flown before and as I sat on the plane waiting for take off it was all a thrill. The props increased in speed, the engines started to whine and along the runway we roared and then just before takeoff all the lights failed, the engines seemed to cut out and we came to an abrupt stop at the very end of the runway. As we were being towed back to the air terminal I wondered if my shipping company had any part of this airline as the ship I had been on was prone to breakdowns! At least at sea if you broke down you had a chance to swim for it, but at 30,000 feet, well! After a couple of hours in the terminal and the engineers had done their thing we all climbed back aboard and had a second go at taking off and this time it all seemed okay. I have never liked flying since and the only way my wife can get me on a plane is after about half a bottle of brandy. On arrival at Schiphol airport I got a taxi and he took me to the shipping agents office which was in the heart of the town, but as it was still early in the day and they weren't open I lugged my cases over to a local cafe and over a couple of cups of coffee watched Rotterdam slowly come to life. Some of the buildings looked fairly new but over all it seemed pretty bare and drab. At 9 o'clock I made myself known to the agents then got a taxi to take me down to the docks and find my new ship. On the way towards the dock area I looked across the River Maas and saw some of the gigantic tankers laying at the oiling berth and the taxi driver pointed out that Rotterdam was about the biggest oil depot in Europe. We arrived at my new home and at a glance I could see the improvement on my last old rust bucket, but even on this one could sense that over the past two years she had done a lot of work and was in need of a good painting. Going aboard I found my new cabin and made myself known to the other cadet who was to be my senior on this trip then went along to the 1st Mate's cabin to report aboard to him. After a cup of tea I changed into my working gear and had a good look around the ship. I was pleased to find that she had an "iron Mike" or automatic steering which was a blessing and would save hours standing behind the wheel also she actually had a radar, but on this trip we wouldn't be keeping a look out for icebergs as I had found out that our destination was the River Plate and that we would be picking up a cargo of grain and some more general cargo. Over dinner that night I met the other officers and the Captain and on first appearance they all seemed okay and fairly sane. Only time would tell! Most of them and the crew had joined the ship in London and had taken her round a couple of ports on the continent, loading general cargo but the cadet I replaced had only left yesterday to have a bit of leave.

The following day at around noon we cast off and headed the 15 miles down the River Maas to the Hook of Holland and out into open waters. I had been on the wheel whilst we made for the seas once more and I found that the wheelhouse on this ship was much larger than the last one which had been the size of a big broom cupboard. It all seemed very modern what with

57

the radar sitting there and the auto helm ready to come into use when asked. Once again we steamed down the Channel, across Biscay and then towards the Canary Isles again. Our first port of call, which would take about nine days was to be the Cape Verde Isles, of which I had never heard of until then and there we would pick up oil, water and a couple of pallets of cargo. I looked up in a book to see what I could find out about these isles and reading about them they didn't seem too inviting. It seemed that they were made up of fifteen volcanic islands with very little water, on the same latitude as Dakor, which meant that it was very hot, and they were somewhere in the Atlantic, well, longitude 25°. The population was only about 326,000 and on arrival there I didn't want to be the next to settle down there either. We anchored in the middle of the inlet and we were surrounded by tall volcanic mountains, with very little vegetation on the sides. As we dropped the hook the heat hit us and for our few hours stay there all on board sweated buckets. I found out later that the film "Brown on Resolution" from C.S. Forrester's book was made here and if you have read it you see that it was the perfect spot. The oil, water and our couple of pallets of cargo were all brought out to us by lighters and we were also surrounded by bum boats with the locals trying to sell us souvenirs and, more important to us, local hooch which was some form of Anisette. They didn't do very well with the souvenirs, but a lot of bottles came aboard, much to our regret the next day. God, it was awful stuff but at the time it tasted quite nice with a bit of ice after the first glass, but why any of us didn't go blind after drinking a lot of it I will never know. The next day everyone was still reeling around as when you had a cup of tea or a glass of water it seemed to have the effect of making you drunk again. Lethal stuff. All on board, when after a few hours the anchor was winched up and we moved out of that hell hole and were once more in open waters and a cool breeze, were more than happy. That's one holiday isle that is definitely off my list.

We headed south once more and I was becoming a little apprehensive as in three days we would be crossing the equator and as it was my first time over the line the crew said that they would give me a special ceremony and that I would finish up being shaved all over and not a hair left on my young body. We approached the equator, we crossed the equator, nothing happened and I was very happy. The weather was wonderful with clear skies and flat blue seas and it was surprising what life you could see from time to time. The porpoise joined us from time to time and played around the bows doing their banging act and also the occasional turtle was to be seen as it flopped through the water to keep clear of the ship. Now and then whales surfaced blowing streams of air and water and to see these giants nearly leap out of the water is some sight to behold. One day on the bridge I saw a disturbance a few hundred feet away from the ship and when I got a pair of glasses to have a closer look it looked like a long thin neck sticking out of the sea and seemed to be having a look around. To this day I don't know what it was and I am sure that the oceans still have a lot of life in them that we don't know about. Just south of the equator we met our first albatross and to me it's the finest seabird with those magnificent great wings and they just seem to glide in the wind and never seem to flap those wings. It's strange that these birds can't seem to live in the northern hemisphere and once you are about 5° south of the equator they turn round and head south again. The other wild life we encountered was the bosuns chickens that he had bought in the Cape Verdi Isles, after a bottle of "that stuff". He was very proud of them and they lived on top of No. 5 hatch in a run he had made for them. Every time that one produced an egg it was celebrations all round and as he wasn't too sure whether he was allowed to take them into South America he did the gentlemanly act and we all had a bit of fresh chicken one Sunday. He was very upset about that, but after a bottle of rum some of us bought for him he soon got over it.

After a further thirteen days steaming we got to the entrance of the Plate and picked up our river pilot as we were going quite a way up to a place called Rosario. The mouth of the Plate is gigantic and about 150 miles across at the seaward end and even at Buenos Aires it is 30 miles wide. We passed Buenos Aires and continued up stream and it would be a long trek as Rosario was about 145 miles and as we were averaging about 8 knots, a long time. At least it was very interesting at the wheel and I had a good view of the pampas, that seemed to stretch forever, also as we got further up the river it got pretty narrow and the trees nearly touched the bridge as we went through the jungle section. It seemed a bit like the "African Queen", as long as we didn't have to get out and pull her! The pilot was a very likeable man and I had some very interesting conversations with him and he gave me some lessons in Spanish or rather the bastardised Spanish they spoke out here. He told me that Rosario was a large city with a university and a big cathedral and the population was about 750,000 people and that the industry was steel and iron and a lot of agriculture. He also said that it stood on the banks of the River Parana not the Plate so bang went my navigation. He asked me all about my home town and I tried to explain about Canterbury and he seemed very interested in it all. What with all the course alterations and our chats time flew and I was sorry when I got relieved at the wheel.

As we approached Rosario we received the good news that it would take about two weeks to get rid of our general cargo and then start loading for our return trip, finishing up in Buenos Aires to top up.

This was my introduction to South America and it always has been my favourite country and the people have always made me feel at home and they were very pro-British. I didn't like the people in power out there and it was not wise to get involved with the police as they were a very hard lot and a lot of people were known to disappear. I have seen when there was a disturbance once, one mounted policeman on one side of the street and another on the other with a large net between them and they galloped down the road and scooped the offenders up in the net causing a lot of injuries. Also outside banks and official buildings they stood there with automatic weapons in their hands and if you got a bit too close to them it was very prudent to step out of the way.

Our unloading berth was close to town so at the end of the working day most on board got changed into civvies and headed up to the centre to have one of the finest steaks you could have dreamt of, a bottle of wine, total cost £1. Whilst we were at this berth the cook just about became redundant as, apart from breakfast everyone ate ashore. For lunch we walked along the quay to a mobile cafe and for a few pence we had a steak sandwich. This was all very pleasant and it's so sad that now with inflation so high out there the locals can't afford to eat steak. After about four days our holds were empty so we had to move to the grain elevator which was about 3 miles out of town and this seemed as though it would interfere with our social life as it would be a taxi job to get to town every night. Depression set in as we all seemed to have made friends with the local girls and a taxi every night would put our costs up. The wharf was in the middle of nowhere and not a bar in sight, but I had a chat with the local night watchman and he said that the local bar was about half a mile away, up a steep track along a disused railway track. How to get there was a problem, but he said no trouble and pointed to the end of the jetty, and there stood our new form of conveyance. The horse! For a few centavos we could hire these and get to the bar. So for the next few nights we would clamber

61

aboard our nags and ride up the hill along the railway and into the bar. Coming back was fun as by then, after a lot of rum, we all thought that we were expert horsemen and took some hairy chances as we galloped back. A few stayed the night as the local girls would, for 200 cigarettes, make you more than welcome. On one night I was a bit late setting off to the bar so I told the rest to ride on and I would catch them up. I rode up the hill and started along the track and by now it was getting quite dark, when suddenly I was surrounded by a group of young men. They rabbited on at me and I had no idea what they were on about when a bloody great knife was stuck in the saddle. I kicked one of them under the chin and got my horse to break into a sort of canter and headed for the bar at the double. After a drink to calm my nerves I asked the barman what that was all about and he said that they didn't mean any harm and they just wanted to give me a knife fight! Charming I thought and from then on we travelled in convoys. As we weren't going to start to load for three days, due to a religious festival, I had a few afternoons off and took advantage and hired one of the horses for long rides into the pampas and had a good look around the local area which was all very fascinating. The saddles were hard and after a couple of hours the bums were sore, but it was fun.

We started to load our grain and the speed that the dockers worked was very civilised and nobody rushed around. Instead of shifting boards to keep the grain stable we had sacks of grain laid on top of the loose cargo and this acted as stabilisers. The tween decks were being kept for other cargo which we would be picking up at Buenos Aires. After ten days we moved the ship to Swifts corned beef factory and we picked up a few hundred tons of bully beef. I became friendly with the manager of the factory and he asked myself and the 2nd Mate if we would like to look around. It was a big factory and as far as we could make out, a cow went in one end and it came out in a tin from the other. I wasn't too impressed to see the animals slaughtered and the smell was much to be desired, but it was all very interesting. Life was very nice, during the day we chipped and painted the ship and at night up to town for the night life and as there was another religious festival for two days it was all at a steady pace with, of course, a long siesta each day. To think that nowadays it only takes a few hours to load a supertanker and very little time ashore, I think the old method was much more civilised. At last we were loaded and with the pilot on board said our sad farewells to Rosario and headed down river.

Buenos Aires, what a city! To me it is a marvellous place with wonderful people. I believe that it is the largest city in the southern hemisphere and has the widest street in the world, but with a population of nearly three million, a third of the total population of the Argentine, what would you expect. Although Peron was in exile in Spain it surprised me that the locals were still in favour of him and to them Eva was still the queen. The girls were beautiful with long black hair and brown eyes and as I have stated before were very pro-British, so we couldn't go wrong, and what a way to learn more Spanish. The main part of the city was very modern with a very large railway station that fed systems to all over Argentina also it had a fine underground network of which I used quite a lot as a couple of my girl friends lived on the outskirts of the city.

It was going to take about eight days to finish loading so the Chief Officer got us cadets and the seamen to paint the sides of the ship. On one day I was on a stage with an A.B. and we had worked out way down to just above the water line when he suddenly gave a yell and shouted "Oh shit!" and started to scramble up the rope to the ships deck. "What's wrong?" I yelled up at him. "Look by your side" he shouted back. I turned round and next to me floating in the water was a man with his throat cut from ear to ear! We didn't fancy steak that night.

And so after another eight days our cargo was aboard and we prepared to go to sea once again. It had been an enjoyable stay and I suppose that one of my claims to fame is that I had to have a tooth out by a dentist in Buenos Aires, and not too many people can say that. We had to anchor outside Buenos Aires for five hours as there was naval exercises going on down the Plate and the old man didn't want to get mixed up in that lot. Once we got clear of the Plate it was back to the old routine and it was pleasant to get into clear waters once again. Our next port of call was to be at St. Vincent which was in the Windward Islands just north of Venezuela and apart from picking up water and oil for our own use we would be loading a few more hundred tons of cargo. It would take about fourteen days to tramp there so back to more studying, but at least I was allowed to take sights with my sextant and try and find the ships noon position. The first time at this we were off the coast of Brazil and when the Captain asked me what position I had made it I put the ship in the middle of the Brazilian rain forest! I did improve in time.

Up the coast of South America we steamed once more crossing the equator, I was getting an old hand at that. When we were just off the coast of French Guiana I saw a small island and when I enquired where it was I was informed that it was a prison island. On reflection I think that it must have been the infamous Devils Island where Dreyfus was imprisoned. Another tropical island off my holiday list. We arrived at Kingston, the capital of St. Vincent, at 14.00 hours and they started to load our few tons of cargo directly, as was the same with the fresh water and bunker oil. No chance to have a look around which was a shame as it looked a very nice place and by 19.00 hours our ropes had been cast off and our bows were then heading in an easterly direction, back towards the U.K. It was only about a nine day run to the entrance to the English Channel and we were waiting for our unloading orders which we would receive when we got there. This was called L.E.F.O., or Lands End For Orders, of which we all hoped that they would be for a port in the dear old U.K. and as we would get there about December 20th, a great chance to have Christmas at home. Sods law took over and when we got our orders it was for Rotterdam and the Captain then informed me that I would be the stand by crew over the Christmas period and no leave at all. When we arrived in Rotterdam we were put on a buoy in the middle of the harbour as the ship wouldn't start to unload until after the New year and with a pretty heavy heart I watched most of the officers and crew being taken ashore to go on leave and have Christmas and the New Year with their families. This left one of the Mates, an engineer and a couple of seamen and greasers and the purser who would be doing all the cooking for us over the festive season. So far I had been on the ship for just under four months and as I was led to believe the next trip would be quite a long one as well, I wouldn't be having some leave for some time to come. Oh well, I thought over a can of beer that evening in the silent ship, I always wanted to see how the continentals spent Christmas.

Chapter 6

West Coast of America

It turned out that the ship didn't leave the continent for just over a month by the time we had discharged our cargo and had gone to a couple more ports to load up for America. Christmas in Rotterdam turned out to be a pleasant time and Christmas Day I spent with the night watchman and his family who I had become friendly with. His large barge was tied up alongside us and it was beautiful inside and very cosy, but as it was his home I suppose it had to be. It was all very pleasant and they treated me like a son and even gave me a pair of fur lined leather boots for a present, which I must say was most welcome as it was damn cold there. In the evenings I used to go to the Flying Angel - Mission to Seamen, as there was always a dance or something on and I got pretty friendly with one of the girls there and asked her out for a date. I thought that it would be a pretty staid affair, but after a meal she took me on a tour of all the back street bars and we then went on to have a look around the red light area, finishing up back at her flat. Christmas present number two! The only thing that marred that period was the death of one of the crew. The engineer officer who had been standing by on the ship had been relieved and was leaving the ship to fly home to his wife and children. The launch that was taking him ashore was cut in half by a large tanker and his body was never found. He had been a pleasant and popular man and our flags flew at half mast for him.

I received my mail from my parents and was horrified to find out that my younger brother, John, had failed to get into Dartmouth, the Royal Naval College, and had decided to join the Merchant Navy as a cadet! Stupid bugger I thought and how proud my parents must have been to have two lunatic sons in the

66

family.   At least he was going into a respectable shipping company with modern ships on a regular run, so maybe I was the only mad one.

We unloaded our cargo of South American grain and by now the new complement of officers and crew were aboard, mostly from London which was good news as they usually were a not too bad lot. We left Rotterdam and moved on to Antwerp to start loading for the States. This was only a short hop. Back down the river to the Hook, then about 50 miles along the flat coast line before turning into the Scheldt river, passing Flushing and then another 45 miles to Antwerp. It is a lovely old town with lots of atmosphere about it, especially at night. The 3rd Mate and I wandered down one night to have a look at the red light area and this was quite an education seeing all the girls sitting in their front rooms displaying all their wares. We went into a small bar and after a couple of drinks we started chatting up a couple of very pretty girls and we were getting on like a house on fire when the ships bosun came staggering in and burst out laughing. He took us to one side and asked if we knew that this was the local gays bar and that the two pretty girls that we had picked up were a pair of young queens and if we had gone any further with them we would have got a shock. We didn't go back for our drinks, but made a mad dash for the exit. Shows you have to be careful.

Our cargo for the States was being loaded and it certainly was all different goods from steel pipes to one hundred cases of continental chocolate which was stowed and secured from our grubby little paws. After a few days we had to move round to Hamburg to finish off loading before departing the continent. This was only another short trip, about 350 miles up the flat coastline before turning into the River Elbe and then a further 60 miles upstream. When we arrived it was pouring with rain so the stevedores couldn't start work and Mike, the other cadet, asked me if I wanted to go ashore and have a look around, but by then I had been about five weeks ashore on the continent and I was sure that there would be another time that I could see what Hamburg had to offer. I was looking forward to getting back to the open sea and a regular routine once again and also with all the times ashore my financial situation by then was at rock bottom. The next day our holds were full and we were once again battened down and took our leave of Hamburg and put our bows into the January gales and headed for the Channel.

Our cargo was destined for Los Angeles and I was looking forward to going through the Panama Canal and all its wonders. The 1st Mate must have taken pity on me for having to stay aboard for Christmas as he put me on day work which meant I didn't have to stand a watch and my hours were from 9-5, office hours. Life was agreeable and once we had passed down the Channel and across Biscay with its strong gales and heavy seas crashing over the bows the weather changed and we got into our shorts. With no watch keeping it meant I got a full nights sleep without being shaken at some godforsaken hour to go on to the bridge and some of the jobs were making cargo nets, making pilot ladders, checking the holds to see if the cargo had shifted, splicing new ropes and wires and many, many more. I did a couple of hours studying each day and I was getting used to using the sextant to <u>try</u> and find the ships position, which I enjoyed. It must be pretty boring nowadays as all you do is press a button and the ships position appears on a screen so a lot of the art of true navigation has been taken away and I think that it is sad. God knows what happens if you have a full power failure or the satellite has gone wrong as I am sure that a lot of sextants stay in their boxes these days and to have to suddenly have to take a sight must be quite frightening, if the navigators remember how to do it.

The ship inevitably broke down a few times due to engines or steering failure and during these times we took up the art of shark fishing. Well, not quite fishing, more of a massacre as our skill was to get a heaving line, fix a meat hook on the end with a large chunk of meat obtained from the cook, the engineers would give us steam on the stern winch and when we got a bite hauled the line in. When we caught one, and some got up to 15 feet, when we got it on deck we all ran like hell as it flapped all over the place with its teeth flashing. I still have a set of one of their teeth which are evil things and one of the crew made a very nice walking stick out of the backbone of one. the cook had this brilliant idea about shark fin soup and set to work to give us all a treat, but it turned out to be vile and finished up back in the sea. It was all a bit of fun and broke the monotony, but I don't think J.R. Hartley would have approved of our methods!

It took us about twenty days to get to Panama and we had to make a detour to Williemstad, which is the capital of Curacoa in the Antilles just off Venezuala, to take on oil and water. From there it was about 800 miles to the entrance of the Panama Canal and on arrival we were told to anchor off and wait our turn which was to be the next day. As we swung at anchor some bright spark suggested that it would be nice to go for a swim and as it was boiling and the sea did look inviting a few of us took the plunge. It was very relaxing and as we swam around the ship the pilot, who had come aboard, shouted down to us didn't we know that there was a lot of alligators around this area. I've never climbed an anchor chain before, but I did that time and the rest of the swimmers got out as fast as I did. It's an amazing place the Panama and as we swung at anchor it was interesting to see all the different ships from all over the world waiting to enter or come out from the Canal. We could see the town of Cristobel, which is the town at the north end of the Canal whilst Panama itself is at the southern end. Panama holds 25% of the total population of the country and I assume that after the year 2000 it will become fairly affluent as they take over the Canal. At the moment the States leases what is called the Panama Canal zone which is a strip of land 8 miles each side of the Canal for its military bases and it also takes 25% of the revenue that the Canal takes. So logically after the States withdraws Panama gets an increase of 25% which must be a hell of a lot with all the shipping passing through. From the Caribbean to the Pacific is about 30 miles and is a series of lakes and locks and it took us eleven hours to get through what with all the waiting to enter the locks and having to slowly move along the waiting jetties. As we entered the first lock the young pantry boy aboard the ship realised that he had been had as for the past few days he had been saving all the old stale bread for the mules that would tow us through the locks. The mules, as they are called, are not our four legged friends, but gigantic diesel engines that tow us along. It was all quite an experience to pass through, but we were all glad to enter the Pacific and start our 3,250 mile trip as it had been a long day and to travel 30 miles in eleven hours was quite monotonous.

The weather remained kind to us as we travelled up the eastern side of the States and after a further eleven days we approached Los Angeles. I was looking forward to my stay there as an uncle of mine lived there and after sending him a telegram from the ship and asking the Captain's permission I was to be let off the ship and stay with him whilst the ship was being unloaded. God, I thought, I hope that there is a dock strike for a week. We got alongside and after we were cleared by customs and health officers, I went to the nearest phone and gave Cliff a buzz and within the hour I was sitting in his car heading for the city centre, much to the jealousy of some members aboard, but sod them I thought with a smile on my face.

As we drove towards Wiltshire Avenue which was 30 miles along the road, Los Angeles or city of angels seemed to go on forever and Cliff said that it was about 60 miles from one end to the other. Cliff and Jill lived in a very nice place and for the next few days I lounged around their swimming pool, watched T.V. and generally relaxed. They took me out in the evenings for dinner and one afternoon Cliff took time off from work and showed me Hollywood, Beverley Hills and the other places of interest. One afternoon I decided to take a walk and have a look at the local sights, but within an hour I had been stopped twice by policemen and asked what I was doing. When I said that I was just going for a walk one of them said "You must be English, don't you know that nobody walks around here." Strange people the Americans and what a blight on their society. My stay was very enjoyable and after four days I had a phone call from the 2nd Mate and was told to rejoin the ship as we would be sailing the next day.

We left Los Angeles with happy memories and made our way up the Californian coast line on our 400 mile hop to San Francisco to clear the rest of our cargo. As we approached that famous bay I climbed to the top of the mast to get some photographs of the Golden Gate Bridge and the picturesque surrounding hilly countryside also to see Alcatraz, the prison, and I could understand why not many prisoners escaped from there as the currents around it were terrible and they wouldn't have much chance to survive in those waters. As we nudged our way alongside our berth I could see steep hills with traffic moving up and down, also the little cable cars going up and down. God, I thought, all we needed now was Tony Bennett to burst into song! Our stay was only for a couple of days, but I did get a chance to have a good look around and I was impressed at how clean the city was, but decided that to live in that hilly city one needed a very strong pair of legs or a very strong clutch in your car. One evening myself and Mike made our way along to the famous Fishermans Wharf and got into the fantastic atmosphere there, all hustle and bustle but at the same time, very laid back. We treated ourselves to a fish dinner and that was out of this world, so was the price, but some experience. So with empty holds we bade farewell to Frisco and put the ships bows north once more for our next port of call was to be Vancouver and Vancouver Island to pick up a full cargo of timber for London. It wasn't too far up the coast, about 900 miles to Cape Flattery before turning into the Sound and Vancouver. The bay and approaches to Vancouver were spectacular with wooded hill sides and a natural harbour which made it all very picturesque. We would be about three weeks here and round the island loading our timber and by the time the holds were full we then loaded a deck cargo to a height just below the bridge house windows and had to have cat walks on the top so we could get to the bows and stern of the ship. The deck cargo was secured by chains and bottle screws to stop the cargo shifting in bad seas so each day all this had to be checked. We only stopped a few days in Vancouver before moving across to Victoria, the capital of the island, and the start of our port hopping around the island. I fell in love with the island and if anyone asked me where I would like to live apart from England, this would be the place.

Victoria itself is a lovely place with a lot of old buildings and the government house is magnificent dating back, I assume, to Victoria's reign. Old London buses were still in use round the town and the telephone boxes were the old red ones that we had in this country. The countryside all around the island is beautiful, hilly and woody which made sense as the main export was timber and most of the houses were wood built. I got to see a lot of the island as this must have been my lucky trip for two of my cousins lived here and the old man gave me a couple of days leave to go visiting. This was great and they showed me around and took me all over the place and then in the evenings out to dinner and a few drinks. The local people overwhelmed us aboard ship with their hospitality and most evenings I would be invited out to one of the locals houses for dinner as were a lot of the officers and crew. In one of the small ports the local indians who were working on the docks asked us to play football so we scrapped a team up of the most fit aboard and gave them a game which caused a lot of local interest. We played to the best of our ability and lost 6 - 0, but it was all fun and we had a big party on board that night to celebrate the fine skills at that sport. As we moved round the small ports, mostly just very large saw mills and a loading jetty, it was fascinating to see the huge log jams being towed along by a small work boat to the mills. New Westminster, Nanaimo, Port Alberni, Cawitchan Bay, these were some of the places we picked up our timber and all made us most welcome. These had been a very agreeable three weeks and I think that nearly all on board were a little sad to say goodbye to this lovely place and I hope that some day I may return to see if it is still as nice as ever.

It was now early April and with our holds and decks full we started on our long trip back to dear old England. The ship looked pretty smart as we had given her a good painting whilst around the island so the Captain was happy which made the rest of us happy as he didn't moan so much. Down the coast of America we tramped and sixteen days later once more went through the Panama, but the ship was not happy then as the agent there said that there wasn't any mail for us so nobody got any letters from home. Things like this get blown out of proportion after you had been at sea a while and some of the crew got pretty nasty. Once through the Canal we then went on to Curacoa to fill our ever hungry fuel tanks and, thank God, we got our mail. We stayed the night there and tied up, astern of us was a smart British ship from a well respected shipping line. Myself and

Mike got invited on board by the senior cadet from the ship so we had a very good meal aboard her and then had a few drinks with the four cadets on her. It was nice to see how the other half lived and when we invited them back to our ship they declined, and I don't blame them after seeing the high standard of their cabins and life style they had. The shipping company I was with was infamous for bad ships and crews so I think that they must have felt sorry for us and wanted to give us a treat for the night. It was all fun and we staggered back to our ship in the early hours to get a few hours sleep before getting under way once again.

Another sixteen days steaming and we entered the Thames estuary and headed up towards Tilbury to start unloading our cargo, but most important was the fact that I was going on leave. It had been eight months since I had trodden on English soil and I must say that the smells and sounds of London were very pleasant indeed. And so with my cases packed and a spring in my step I left the ship and made my way to the station and some well earned leave before rejoining another ship and be heading off to another part of the world.

Chapter 7

Sugar and Coal

My expected long leave in fact lasted ten days and to me it didn't seem very fair to have been at sea eight months and only get that amount of time at home. The telegram arrived so I had to pack my bags and rejoined the ship in London as I couldn't argue with my lords and masters. When I got aboard Mike, the other cadet, packed his bags and headed off for a few days leave as he had been standing by whilst most of the cargo had been discharged. The second day I was aboard my parents came up to the ship to see what the ship was all about and after a tour of inspection I'm not sure what they thought but they left in a quiet mood and didn't say too much. I don't think it was what they had in mind and not the greyhound of the sea they thought. That evening after dinner I went up west to see a film and that is when I got one of my bouts of malaria and finished up in Charing Cross hospital for a few days. As luck would have it I was discharged from the hospital the day before the ship was due to sail so I had to rejoin her and not go home for a few days rest.

We left London a light ship and we were going to Casablanca to pick up a cargo for South Africa and then Burma. It was to be coal this time, not a nice clean cargo that we had just got rid of and the Captain was already worrying about his nice clean ship. At least we didn't have to do any bilge cleaning before picking the cargo up as the timber didn't effect the bilges, but the coal would. It only took a few days to get to Casablanca, or El Dar-El-Deida as it is called and as we moored alongside the coal berth the heat hit us like a furnace. We got alongside at 3pm and started loading straight away and continued until 11pm that night and by then I was completely worn out as I still hadn't got over my malaria totally and collapsed on my bunk to get a few hours sleep. Work started again at 8am and by noon our holds were full and we moved out to anchor to cover the hatches, drop the derricks and wash all the coal dust off the ship. Everything was covered in a black coat of dust and everything that you ate or drank tasted of coal, but at least it wasn't as bad as that sulphur, thank God. Once again we headed out to sea and our direction was for Dakar to pick up oil and water for our trip south towards the Cape.

A few days out I was on the bridge with the 2nd Mate when we saw something strange in the water ahead of us so the Captain was called. As we got closer we saw it was a lifeboat full of men and they were waving to us, so the engine room was informed and we slowed down until when they were alongside we stopped engines. After a lot of shouting up to us they explained in broken English that they were Brazilian deserters and they were trying to get to the Canary Isles. What they had deserted from and how they got to where they were we never found out, but after giving them the course they wanted and as they didn't want anything else from us we got under way again and the last we saw of them was as they raised their small sail and set off on the course that we had given them. I wonder what story they could have told us and if they ever got to their destination.

Dakar came and went and we only stayed for about six hours for our oil and water, but in that time Mike, my cabin companion managed to purchase a set of Bongo drums! Over the next couple of days he drove me and a lot of other people mad with his drumming on the damn things. A few of us had a serious meeting and it was Mike or the drums had to go and as he was a nice chap one night, when he was on watch, the drums vanished over the ships side much to Mike's disgust. We all returned to sanity. I had been studying hard as my yearly exams were due and under the watchful eye of the Captain I had a week of papers to sit, maths, navigation, ships construction, electricity, science and seamanship to name but a few and by the end of the week I was glad it was all over and that I had done fairly well with a passable result. I had exams each year so at least I could relax for a while but I still had to study each day. We still were forever painting the cable locker with red lead. The cable locker is a small sort of hatch where the anchor chain lives and that was a terrible job as the red lead fumes just about knocked you out after about thirty minutes painting. The 1st Mate didn't like me and I didn't like the 1st Mate. I was the one to have to paint the top of the mast, one moment over the ship the next over the sea as the ship rolled, getting more paint over me than the actual mast. I was the one to crawl along the top of the coal down the hatches with a torch to fumble my way through the pitch black to make sure all was okay down there. I didn't like the 1st Mate.

Our trip to Durban was about 4,800 miles or about twenty days steaming as long as the engines kept going and nothing fell off. When we were off Cape Town I could see Table Top Mountain and to me it looked just like a long hill with a flat top. Sorry I can't be romantic about it. We passed the Cape of Good Hope and along the bottom of Africa with another 950 miles to go before we got to Durban.

Durban is a lovely place and I had a great time ashore there as did most on board. My friend Mike fell in love there and eventually she came back to England and they got married. I fell in love many times there but didn't bring any of them back home. The beaches are beautiful with miles of golden sands and a lovely warm sea. A crowd of us used to go to the beach quite often, swimming and having drinks in the beach bars, until one day we got thrown off. One of the crew was called Sharky and one time he was happily playing around in the water we wondered if he would like another drink so about four of us stood up and shouted "Sharky, Sharky". People screamed and the water cleared as there was a mad panic to get up the beach and away

77

from the sea. Crowds gathered and we couldn't understand why people were pointing towards the sea and saying "Where? Where?" A very big lifeguard came up to us and asked where we had seen the shark! We then realised that sharks sometimes visited the beaches round that area and that we had started a panic. During the chaos we managed to get dressed and slip away before we got hung, drawn and quartered. We didn't go to that beach again, but found one the other end of town. The main part of the town seemed pretty modern with high rise offices towering over the streets. It was nice to mingle with the throngs all going to and from their work and after the fairly peaceful existence aboard ship it was a pleasant feeling to be jostled by the swarms of people. I could never get used to the definite line between blacks and whites and to see all the signs 'No Whites' or 'No Blacks' on buses, bars, toilets and just about everything was all beyond me. I know that if a white man was caught in bed with a black girl the sentence was something like ten years hard labour so we all stuck to the rules, but this wasn't too hard to do as the white, local girls were very pretty and very willing. The police were, I assume, Afrikaan and they looked big and tough and not to be crossed so we kept out of their way. Durban is the only place in the world that I have been ice skating and I put this down to three quarters of a bottle of Cape Brandy. I found it hard to stand up on the ice and this I put down to that I was not born a natural ice skater and the second reason was the Brandy.

After about six very pleasant days we had discharged about half our coal and the remaining cargo was for Rangoon and after trimming the hatches and battening down we took our leave of Durban, hoping to return on another trip. We left 02.00 hours in the morning and as I was then put on the 4-8 watch got my head down for two hours before going on watch again. The 1st Mate still had a grudge towards me and after I came off watch he told me to check each hold to see if things were all okay. I armed myself with a torch and climbed down the ladder into the dark of No. 1 hold and had a long look around the tween decks and shone the torch down onto the coal in the main hold. I saw what I thought was a bundle of rags in a corner so I jumped down on to the coal and crawled my way across to see what it was. I grabbed hold of the rags and gave a tug and the next thing I saw was a pair of open eyes staring at me and they belonged to a black man who was as dead as a dodo. I got out of there as quick as I could and did a runner to the bridge to report my find. It transpired that he was one of the dockers from Durban and must have fallen down the hold and not been seen. I still can't remember what we did with the body, but we didn't have a burial at sea!

From Durban to the mouth of the Irrawaddy River was about 5,000 miles or about three weeks that we hoped the prop would keep turning. We passed the bottom of Madagascar up through the Indian Ocean and made our way to the Gulf of Martaban which is where the leg of the Irrawaddy joins the ocean. Rangoon stands on this section of the river whereas the main delta of the river runs into the Bay of Bengal. When we had picked up the pilot and I was at my place on the wheel we started our way up the river towards Rangoon and I thought this was not my favourite river as logs, trees, dead cows, huts, bodies and lots of unmentionable things floated pass us. The heat was oppressive and the smell much to be desired and I thought that if this was the magic east, keep it. We nosed the ship alongside the coal berth and I prayed that the 1st Mate wouldn't have me over the ship side painting as to get near the water line was the last thing that I wanted.

The hatch covers remained on that afternoon and no cargo was discharged so myself and a couple of others walked up to the town to see the mysteries of the east. We were not impressed with the open sewers that ran along the side of the road and the smell wasn't too nice, but we managed to find the Golden Temple and to see the whole roof covered in gold is a sight to behold. There was pagodas all over the place and to find a fairly reasonable bar was quite a task but like all good British seamen we won in the end. We were very careful what we drank as the standard of hygiene was much to be desired and to go to the loo was a real test of nerves. We started to get into the spirit of the Far East and I went and had my fortune told by the local soothsay and it looked a rosy future for me apart that he said that one person was gunning for me. How did he know about the 1st Mate! We looked at the local restaurants, but decided that our stomachs were not yet prepared for what was on offer and decided to go and take our chances with the cook aboard our ship, at least we knew how bad that was. After I got back aboard and was settled in my cabin with an ice cold beer the 1st Mate staggered in, he had been on the bottle, and with a crooked smile on his face told me that I was to be the night watchman for the next three nights. Bastard, I thought, no sleep that night. Apart from myself as the night watchman one of the local Burmese was also on duty to stop persons not permitted to come aboard. Him and I became quite friendly and at about 2am I gave him a cup of tea and he shared his dinner with me. This was the best curry I have ever tasted in my life and although it was cold and wrapped in bamboo leaves it was also the hottest curry I have ever had the pleasure to eat. A super meal. I used to get to my bunk at about 07.00 and get up at about 2pm and after getting into my civvies I walked up to an English club which let us have the use of their lovely swimming pool and after half an hours swim, lounged alongside the pool with some form of iced drink in my hand, chatting up the local English girls who lived out there. This was a civilised way of life and I could have got used to it, but as the sun started to set I had to return to the ship to make sure that it was not stolen in the night.

I think that the worst aspect out there was the humidity and after doing the smallest task you would be wringing with sweat and even after a change of clothing you still felt damp and sticky. It also rained a lot which didn't help things and I think that we were all glad when the last of our black gold had been taken from our deep holds and we were ready to make our way to the clean cool ocean. Our last rope was cast off and our bows turned in the muddy waters and we steamed back down the Irrawaddy, still surrounded by things floating all around us, and made for the open sea. Once clear of the heavy shipping area we tried to put on the automatic steering, but that seemed to have broken down so that meant hand steering until the engineers could sort out the problem and this took five days. Our next destination was Mauritius and we were going to pick up a full cargo of sugar which meant that over the next few days all the holds had to be cleaned of the coal dust, also the bilges had to be emptied. The 1st Mate was in his element and had us working fourteen hours a day to clean the holds and it wasn't the height of laughs to crawl into the bilges with a bucket scooping out all the remains of our last cargo and after a couple of days we looked more like coal miners than British seamen and if we weren't down the holds or on watch we were trying to keep up with washing our clothes. The 1st Mate was in his element and walked around with a fixed grin on his face and the more I thought about it the more I thought he must have had a relation on the Bounty. My eighteenth birthday came and went and I wondered if I was a year wiser, decided not and got on with my washing and ironing. For eleven days we cleaned the holds and in that time we had steamed about 3,750 miles and we were very glad to anchor up in Port Louis harbour and have the evening off and apart from the anchor watch we all got pissed! The following morning I was on anchor watch on the bridge and the old man came up and flopped in his Captain's chair. "Biddick" he said to me, "remember two things about Port Louis; there are sharks in the harbour and syphilis in the town." Charming I thought as he left the bridge after passing this piece of advice to me, I suppose the moral is don't fall in the harbour and be careful where you put it ashore. Looking ashore whilst we swung at our anchor it looked a lovely place and outside the town I could see the long expanses of golden beaches that stretched for miles. Mauritius is a volcanic island and is surrounded by coral reefs and that day the weather was beautiful, but this part of the Indian Ocean is prone to cyclones and Mauritius has had quite a few nasty ones. When I went ashore I was surprised by the many different races that live there and some of the girls were gorgeous, I assume by all the mixed blood in them, but the Captain's words always rung in my head so I was a good boy there. 95% of their export trade was sugar so our little ship was doing its thing for the local economy.

The next day at about midday we saw the pilot cutter chugging towards us and as soon as the pilot was on the bridge we hauled up the anchor and made our way to the loading berth. We were told that we wouldn't start loading until the next day so myself and the 2nd Engineer went ashore to explore. Port Louis wasn't much to write home about, but it had lots of atmosphere and many strange smells. After we had wandered around for about an hour we got a local bus to take us out of town and have a look at part of the island. I can see why it's such a popular holiday resort as it's pretty close to paradise with long golden beaches with palm trees surrounding them and crystal clear blue seas. The locals were very friendly and couldn't do enough for us or be more helpful. Part of our tour took us to the bottom of Signal Mountain which is quite famous for something, but for the life of me I can't remember what!

It took us five days to load our sweet cargo and each night I went ashore and partook of the superb restaurants local dishes which were great and at a reasonable price also, I got involved in the night life which was terrific. As I have said the girls were beautiful and when I was chatting one up or they were getting friendly with me and temptation reared its head those damn words of the Captain came floating back to me and I somehow managed to control myself. Some of the crew didn't and after a few days when we were back at sea they had to pop along to see the chief steward, who was supposed to be the medic aboard, and get a jab of penicillin to clear up their little bit of trouble. Yes, we had some pleasant times ashore in Port Louis and during the days we were back to painting the sides of the bloody ship again. I know that at the end of my cadetship I would qualify and get my 2nd Mates ticket, but I suppose it was nice to have a second string to my bow as I am sure that I would also come out as a master painter after all the hundreds of miles I would have painted during my four years.

The holds were full of our cargo of tooth decay, we had swung the beams back into position, covered the hatches and dropped the derricks and once again we were ready to head for sea and back to dear old Britain, but we were sorry to leave our paradise island. From Mauritius our course was for Port Elizabeth which is at the base of Africa and then we hugged the coast in a westerly direction before turning into Cape Town for more oil for the engines. As usual we would only be staying for a few hours so no time for a run ashore. We were nestled up under Table Top Mountain and close up it was pretty big with warships, mainly British and American, and I found out that it was a large naval base for both countries. Four hours later we let go the ropes and started our trek northwards and once again that place Dakar for more oil and water. I reckon that fuel oil must be very cheap there judging by the amount of times we had called in and I wondered if the shipping company had shares in the place. It took us about fourteen days to get there and the ship behaved well with no breakdowns or bits falling off. Usual routine of watch keeping, studying, other different tasks and, of course, the endless painting. The weather was good to us and apart from the heat it was a nice trip. At Dakar we found out that there was no mail for us which meant that it was in the U.K. waiting for us or still in Mauritius, which wasn't too good for the ships moral and the shipping agent nearly got hung when he came on board without our news from home. From Dakar we were making for Greenock in Scotland to discharge our cargo and funnily enough this was the port where this ship and the others in the company were registered. Once past the Canary Islands the weather started to get worse and for the first time for a long time our knees got covered up as we changed from our whites back into our blue uniforms. It was an eleven day trip passing up the west coast of England before putting our bows into the Firth of Clyde and picking up the Greenock pilot to take us into the port. Once we were secured alongside, myself and Mike were informed that we would have to stand by the ship whilst it was being unloaded and then she would be going up the river to Glasgow to have a dry dock. Most of the officers went on leave and the crew signed off so it just left a few of us aboard, but one good thing was that the 1st Officer had gone on leave so that got him off our backs. It took nine days to unload and this period was pretty boring as there wasn't much to do and we were more or less left to our own devices. I went ashore a few nights to see what was what, but I wasn't very impressed with the place and Saturday nights there is a thing to behold as I don't think I have seen so many drunks on the streets, all trying to stay vertical and hanging on to lampposts. It was a pity it wasn't like my little port Burntisland, but it was as different as chalk to cheese. Our cargo was finally gone and we moved the ship up river to Glasgow and slipped into the dry dock and watched the water gush out from under her and once again she was high and dry and the dockers could get on with their repairs. Mike and I packed our bags and left the ship not knowing if we would return to this ship or another one in the company. As he lived in Margate we travelled down to London together and changed trains for the Kent coast, after having a couple of drinks in town. We arranged to meet up in a few days time as he only lived about 20 miles from me, but the main thing was that our leave had started and we could have a few days sanity before being summoned once again and heading to some other part of the world.

Chapter 8

The day the prop fell off

After twenty seven happy days home on leave I was off to join my next ship which was laying at Birkenhead and loading a part cargo for the States. This was a fairly new ship built in 1954, gross tonnage about 5,000 tons, but when I first saw her she looked well used and had rust streaks all over her and was in need of a good coat of paint. Great! Mike, the cadet from the last ship wasn't joining this one, but the cadet already aboard seemed a nice block when I first met him and had been on this ship about a year, hence he looked drawn and haggard. We would be here about ten days loading and as the days moved along the officers and crew started to come aboard and they seemed to be a mixed bunch. This was going to be an interesting trip as the Captain was a renowned drunkard as was the Chief Engineer and Chief Officer. The crew were not much better, a lot with bad discharges from other ships and I know that one of them had just come out of prison for manslaughter. Quite a ships company. I enjoyed my stay in Liverpool and managed to go to a few night clubs and coffee bars and get absorbed in the swinging sixties scene and it was all a lot of fun.

With our hatches half full with general goods we were due to sail on 14th November, but severe gales round the British coastline delayed us for a couple of days, but when the gales went down to a force 8 we departed and made our way down the Mersey and out to the open seas. An hour after clearing the bar the engines decided to break down and for two hours we wallowed and rolled, whilst the engineers did their thing and put things back together. God did we roll and everything got flung all over the place. I know the saying is one hand for the ship and one for yourself, but in this instant it was two hands for yourself

86

and bugger the ship. Down in my cabin everything was in a pile on the deck. Clothes, books, the lot all in a pile. Even when we got under way the wind had come up again to a force 9 and the ship was making really heavy going of it with heavy seas thundering along the decks as she took great big green backs over the bows. I had an uneasy feeling about this ship and this trip. Our first port of call was to be Tampa in Florida where we would discharge our half cargo before moving round to Savannah in Georgia to pick up a full cargo of iron ore for Italy. Our trip into the Atlantic was not very nice and we had life lines rigged up on the desks so that you didn't get swept overboard by the sea running along the decks, but at least we couldn't work on deck so our jobs were at least out of the weather. As usual we had to stop off somewhere for bunkers and it made a change that it wasn't Dakar, but this time it was the Azores, an island some-where in the middle of the Atlantic and as usual we only stayed a few hours while they pumped in our fuel oil. I had to work with the carpenter dipping the fresh water tanks and filling them up to make sure that we didn't run out of water for the Captain's Scotch. The Azores are volcanic islands and they lay about 750 miles from Lisbon and are in the middle of nowhere and not a place to stay for too long. We didn't and after a few hours we were tramping west again and at least the weather had improved and the ship was charging along at 14 knots which seemed a bit foolhardy to me as I was sure at that speed something would fall off or break. I don't know if the Captain was going for the blue riband, but each day we kept that speed up the old man and the Chief Engineer used to celebrate with a bottle of Scotch and once that was gone they used to celebrate that they had just drunk a bottle of Scotch! The crew were a hard lot, but I used to get on with them okay. One of them had this party trick which was pretty disgusting, and I think very dangerous. We would be sitting in the crews mess having a cup of coffee or tea when this guy would shout "lights". The curtains would be drawn over the porthole, he would drop his trousers and as he passed wind he would set fire to it causing a blue flame. God, I thought, I wonder what would happen if he had a flash back! This was a ship of looneys.

We passed through the Florida Straits and steamed up the west side of Florida making for Tampa Bay and our destination was then in sight. It's all pretty flat and boring scenery around there as we went alongside to start discharging. As we only had half a cargo to unload and the Americans worked flat out to get us away there was no chance to go ashore and look around so it was a quick turn around. Our holds empty we cast off and the pilot took us out of the harbour and got aboard his cutter to take him ashore and at that moment the engines decided to break down. Panic set in as we started to drift back towards Tampa, but the engineers managed to get some power going and we crawled out to safety and dropped the anchor while they sorted it all out. I still had this nasty feeling about this ship. From Tampa we went down the western side of Florida, through the straits and then up the other side, making our way towards Savannah, Georgia. During this little trip the ships log went missing, not the one you wrote in, but the one that streamed from the stern to tell you how many miles the ship had travelled. Whether a shark had taken a fancy to it or whether it just fell off I don't know, but I had to construct a new one which wasn't too hard to do and at least I got a pat on the back for it and was asked to join the old man in his cabin to have a Scotch with him. From the northern end of the strait to Savannah was about 350 miles about thirty six hours steaming and as the last cargo we had was clean we didn't have to clean the holds or bilges, thank God. Our port was only a few miles up the River Savannah and we got there at 08.00 and the 5,000 tons of ore started to be shot into our holds and as it wasn't going to take too long to load there was no shore leave for any of us and by 18.30 that was it and we were on our way down river once more. There must have been a naval base there because as the ship moved down stream we saw a lot of warships at anchor all in moth balls, a sort of graveyard for the Navy. We cleared the river and headed east and that was the last we saw of land for the next eighteen days and that was to be the rock as we passed Gibraltar and made our way to Savona.

Life took on its boring routine broken by Christmas Day and the catering staff putting themselves out and producing a decent meal and the old man supplying us with drinks. During the crossing at least the iron mike behaved itself and I didn't have to spend hours steering the damn thing and we only broke down once more for a couple of hours. My use of the sextant was improving and I was starting to take correct sights and put the ship on or near the true position and not in the middle of Trafalgar Square. For December the weather was surprisingly good to us and apart from a few rough days it was a fairly smooth crossing and we averaged a good speed. We passed through the Straits of Gibraltar on 30th December and got to Savona on 2nd January, and it took six days to get rid of the iron ore. We went ashore and celebrated a belated New Years Day and as I had been here before I knew where to go and met up with some of my old friends and was welcomed back in the typical Italian way and they made my stay there very enjoyable, especially a couple of the girls of whom I renewed our friendship. A good way to see the New Year in. As it was the New Year my wages went up. I'm not saying that as a cadet it was cheap labour, but I was now earning the princely sum of £210 per year, or to put it another way, about £4 per week. I know that things were cheaper in those days and that whilst at sea you couldn't spend much, only on bonded goods and things like washing powder, but £4 wasn't really over the top. I still managed to save a bit for home leave and runs ashore, but how I managed I will never know. At least when I was sailing as 3rd and 2nd Mate the increase was staggering and I felt quite rich then.

Our holds empty, many hangovers later and a promise to return to marry that beautiful Italian girl, we departed Savona and headed on a short trip towards Casablanca to pick up another cargo of coal for South Africa and Burma. It took about four days to get there and then once again we were under the coal elevators and the black stuff was being poured into our holds and at the same time covering everything with a nice layer of coal dust. Twenty fours hours later and coughing up coal dust we were back to sea and washing down the decks to try and clean the ship up a bit, but it took a few days and many gallons of water before the ship was anywhere near clean. South, south, forever south, stopping at you know where for a few hours to take on more oil and water before tramping on towards the Cape. No wonder the ship kept breaking down as it seemed that we were forever on the move and that prop shaft kept turning and turning, we hoped. Our first port of call on the Cape was Cape Town and as no one seemed in a hurry to get out the quota for there it took us ten days before we moved on. I had some fun ashore there and remember one night myself and one of the engineers made our way to a bar called "Del Monico's" which was a huge place and packed out as both the American fleet and the royal Navy were both in port. A fight broke out and it was just like in a western with bodies, glasses, tables and chairs all flying through the air in all directions. The funny thing was we sat at our table in the middle of it all just drinking away and when we had finished we put down our glasses on the table, stepped over a few bodies and walked out without even a scratch. Back aboard the Captain had got into a serious drinking session and had got the 2nd Mate involved so for the next few days I had to take over as

3rd Mate while the 3rd Mate took over from the 2nd Mate. All very confusing.

Three days later I went down with another bout of malaria and the doctor that came aboard said that I would have to go to hospital if I didn't improve in the next two days, but on his next visit I had improved a bit so I just stayed in my bunk for the next few days. It was all happening here. After our ten day stay we moved out of Cape Town and worked our way along the coast line another 1,000 miles to Durban. During this little trip the old man was still on a bender and not getting any better. He called me to his cabin one morning at about 10 o'clock and with a glass of Scotch in his hand started asking me navigation questions. Two glasses later he kicked my arse out of his cabin saying I knew F.A. and should work harder and then consoled himself by having a refill. Strange man. We docked at Durban and it was nice to be back and renew old friendships and make new ones. One of the places I used to go to was the Officers Club and here I met a lovely girl and started taking her out. On the second night she invited me back to her flat and she explained that she lived there with her mother who that night was being taken out by this very nice man who was also in the Navy. In the early hours of the morning I heard the front door open and in came mother with her boyfriend. My jaw dropped, his jaw dropped for standing before me was the Captain of the ship! From that moment on I had him, as I had met his wife back in the U.K. His whole attitude to me changed for the rest of the trip and life aboard became a little easier, but it didn't alter his drinking habits. I think the only time he ever stopped drinking was when we were nearing Britain or possibly nearing his wife.

We had a pleasant stay whilst we were there and once again nobody seemed in too much of a hurry to push us back to sea so it was ten days in all that we stayed. I went to see Mike's girlfriend and she told me that she would be going to England soon and that they hoped to get married in the near future. Silly sod, I thought, still she had a very nice friend of whom I became closely involved with and I don't know if she was after a trip to England, but I know I didn't offer. So it was back to sea with the rest of the coal, about half the cargo, for dear old Rangoon and we hoped not a long stay there. I was put on day work again so at least it meant a full nights sleep. One night I didn't. It was just after midnight and I was fast asleep when there was a thumping on my cabin door and it was the 1st Mate telling me to get dressed as quick as I could and get down to the ships stern. I flung on some clothes and at the double raced to the stern of the ship to see the old man and the Chief Engineer both pissed out of their brains shouting at each other. "Something bloody wrong Chief, the engines are going but we are not moving" the old man shouted. "Of course not" shouted back the Chief. "Your f------ propeller has fallen off!" By then some engineer had the sense to stop engines before the whole lot seized up. By now most of the deck crew were up and at the stern and the bosun was rigging up arc lights over the stern of the ship to see if anything could be seen, such as a prop floating around? A pilot ladder had been hung over the stern and the old man told me to climb down it then dive down to see if I could see what was left down there. Charming, I thought, as I stripped to my underpants and started climbing down the ladder, I like swimming, but not that much and this time of the morning in the Indian Ocean. At the bottom of the ladder I took a big breath and dived down as it was quite a way down. The water was warm and with the help of the arc lights I could see fairly well, but what I couldn't see was the propeller and all that was left was the boss where the prop joined the shaft. I rose to the surface and climbed back on to the deck to give my report. As I stood on the deck I could see the huge Scottish bosun grabbing hold of the Captain and shaking him till his teeth nearly fell out. "I will log you for that bosun" yelled the old man, but the bosun just dragged him to the ships side and told him to look down into the water. We all moved to the ships rails and peered down into the clear, floodlit waters. Four huge fins were cruising around the bottom of the ladder and under those four huge fins were four huge sharks! When the ship had stopped and the lights put over the stern this attracted these beauties and how the hell I wasn't inside one I will never know. The Captain looked at me, I looked at him and not much was said. I gave my report about what I hadn't found down there and the officers went to the bridge to have a council of war to take the best action. Every ship carries a spare prop which is usually carried in one of the tween decks and I have read once in a case like ours the spare was put on by shifting the cargo to the forward of the ship so the stern rises out of the water, the spare prop is hoisted over the stern and lowered into position, securely fixed and they went merrily on their way. So all we had to do was to move about 2,000 tons of coal to the bows with shovels and there you are! This was not the answer.

We were about 100 miles off Ceylon and for the rest of the day we drifted while the radio waves were becoming pretty hot. A ship of our size with half a cargo of coal was worth a lot in salvage and I assumed that Lloyds of London were seeing which ships were in the vicinity and what price a tow. The whole ship was in a sort of limbo with none of the usual noises such as the sound of the engine and the swish of the sea being pushed aside by our bows, but it was replaced by creaks and groans from the ship hull and other strange sounds. We still stood our watches, but we weren't going anywhere. During the day we had the job of unsecuring the anchor from the anchor chain as the chain would be part of the towing operation. Night came and still we drifted and we all thanked God that the sea was as flat as a pancake or that we weren't in a busy shipping lane as that would have caused some fun. The sun came up over the horizon and I could see that we had been joined by three ships that were circling us a bit like a shark waiting for its pray, but in this case it was pay. The radio officer was now working for his money and the air waves were full of signals to us and from us also from ship to ship. He at last came to tell the Captain that one of our circling friends had been selected to give us a tow and the ship would be approaching us in about thirty minutes time. I got hold of a pair of the bridge glasses and had a close look at our rescuer and could see that they had unshackled their anchor and were dragging the chain down to the stern of the ship, not an easy job as it weighed a ton. The ship slowly approached astern of us and when she was abeam of us as close as she dared they fired a rocket over our bridge with a line attached to it. This we grabbed hold of and took it up to the forecastle and tied it on to our towing wire of which the other end was shackled to our anchor chain. The ship slowly moved ahead of us and started to winch in our wire and once it was aboard they then shackled it to their anchor chain, so between the ships it was chain, wire, chain, the chain acting as a sort of buffer and taking the strain off the wire so, with a bit of luck, it wouldn't snap. I was called to take the wheel and the ship ahead started to take up the slack and move slowly ahead with us in tow. I was told to steer for the ships stern so that we didn't start veering all over the place and putting strain on the towing wire. This was hard work and took a lot of concentration and after two hours, the end of my spell at the wheel, I was mentally exhausted. We were under way and making for Colombo on the western side of Ceylon and it took us until 7 o'clock the following evening to get there which was an average of about 4 knots which wasn't too bad. On the part of the Captain of the towing vessel he had done a brilliant job and a fine piece of seamanship from start to finish and everyone on our ship took their hats off to him. As we approached Colombo harbour we dropped our anchor about half a mile outside in a safe anchorage and then winched in our tow wire and gave our rescuer a wave as he gave us a couple of blasts on his whistle before heading out to sea again and to continue his voyage. So with a sigh of relief we laid at our anchor and wondered what the next move would be in this game. To cap it all we had run out of fresh water so we were on rations and had to go down to the engine room every time you wanted a cup of water. I suppose that the old man had to drink his Scotch neat, poor sod.

At 09.30 the next morning two tugs came out to us to take us into the harbour, but by now the wind had come up and after two hours trying to tow us they gave up and we had to drop the hook again and wait until the weather abated. That wasn't until two days later and then the pilot came out to us and with the aid of the tugs managed to get us into the inner harbour and safely tied up alongside a quay. A couple of divers came to the stern of the ship and went down to ascertain the damage and they also confirmed that there wasn't a prop there, as if we needed telling. Thirty six days we stayed there whilst a new prop was made in Scotland and shipped out to us and that was a long boring thirty six days. After a few days we had seen what our host town had to offer and we weren't too impressed and found it a rather noisy dirty place with not a lot of night life to see. In the afternoons a few of us went up to a British club which had a very nice swimming pool of which they let us use also a pleasant bar of which we also used, but after a while it became boring there. I managed to talk the 1st Mate into letting myself and a couple of other officers have the use of the lifeboat with the motor in it and we spent a few very nice afternoons motoring out of the harbour and found a lovely deserted beach of which we landed and had a cool swim and a few beers that we managed to bring along with us, those were happy times. Some evenings we went up to the Flying Angel as there was usually a dance or a film show or some form of entertainment for us and the padre who ran the place was a smashing man well down to earth, but dealing with seamen all the time he had to be. After we had been there a couple of weeks he was due to retire and he invited us up to his going away party, which turned out to be a very pleasant affair until towards the end of the evening our Captain, 1st Mate and the 3rd Mate all burst in, pissed out of their brains. God, I thought, these are some of the senior officers of our ship, what a bloody lot. The padre took it well, but the rest of us were well embarrassed and gave our humble apologies for our ship-mates behaviour. On one Sunday a crowd of us caught a bus and went up to Kandy which is about 50 miles inland and one of the main tourist attractions and it was well worth the trip to see the temple of the tooth and see the display by the Kandy dancers, with the ever throbbing beat of the drums. It was quite a day out that. Of course when we were there it was still Ceylon, but from 1972 it became Sri Lanka and I must say with all the change of names of countries worldwide, I should think that geography at school these days must be a nightmare.

Life passed slowly and it seemed that every job we did we did half heartedly and time hung on our hands. One of the daily tasks I had to do was take the temperatures in the holds to make sure that it wasn't getting too hot down there as spontaneous combustion could occur with the coal still in her and I should think that the last thing we wanted was a fire aboard or an explosion. If it got too hot down there we took off a couple of hatch covers to allow it to cool off a bit. Whenever a British ship tied up near to us, myself and James would go aboard and find the cadets and relate the story of our misfortune and this was usually worth a few beers from our listeners and if we were lucky, a decent meal with them as well.

At last our new prop arrived and we were pushed and shoved into the dry dock to have it fitted and this only took a few hours so once more ready, and very willing to head for the open seas again and continue on our way to Rangoon. It was very nice to be back in the open waters and to hear the normal sounds of the ship again, especially the engine working properly. We rounded the base of Ceylon and our course took us in a north easterly direction and we once more headed for Burma, which would take about four days steaming. This was to be nearly the second disaster of the trip. The Captain and some of the Mates were on the bottle to celebrate us being at sea again and believe it or not they got lost and couldn't find the mouth of the Irrawaddy! We should have gone to anchor at the mouth of the river at 07.00 on the fourth day, but no, we steamed up and down the coastline of Burma most of the day trying to find out where we were. We almost run aground on a sandbank and eventually got to our destination at 16.30, only nine hours of cruising around. What a ship this was! That night the Mate went down with a fever, or maybe a nervous breakdown, and I was told to stand his anchor watch which was from 04.00 until 08.00 and just after that the pilot came on board and we started up river and got alongside at 18.00 which made it a very long day and I was glad to fall into my bunk and get out of this mad world for a few hours.

Our stay in Rangoon was for six days whilst the cargo was discharged and it wasn't much fun as I spent most of the time on board. The Mate was still down with his fever and the 3rd Mate and Captain were once again on the bottle, this time I suppose to celebrate the fact that we got here, so I was left to do most of the cargo watches and by the time the evening came I was too tired to bother to get changed and go ashore.

The cargo was out, the hatches covered and we were ready to make our move towards the sea once more. The 2nd Mate had by now gone down with some horrible illness so I was told to stand his watch and I must say that I did enjoy it for the next two days, but as soon as he was up again I was back down again into the bilges scooping out all the filth and cleaning them ready for the sugar that would be poured into us when we got back to Mauritius, if we got back to Mauritius. Another 3,750 mile trek with lots of work in the sixteen days to get the holds ready for our cargo. So back into Port Louis for a week and some more pleasant times ashore before pointing our bows towards the Cape and then north and a homeward course. On this trip the old man made me up to 4th Officer which meant that I stood a watch with the 1st Mate and was giving me some bridge experience, chart work and navigation and as my time as a cadet was soon to come to an end it was a good experience and gave me confidence. I think that the main reason was that the old man wanted someone around in case one of the Mates went down with alcoholic poisoning. We crossed the equator on 18th November and were heading once more for Dakor and the usual top up of oil. One of the crew members, Nick the Greek, went down with very bad stomach pains about three days out from Dakor and by the time we got there he was in a bad way and as soon as we got alongside he was rushed off to hospital and that was the last we saw of him as our stay there was only a few hours. So north again and as usual at that time of the year the weather turned nasty again and all work on the decks was stopped as it was too dangerous to work outside. As we approached the Bay of Biscay the Captain stopped drinking and went on his drying out period as he soon would have to face his wife as well as the shipping company's people. He drank very little when in the U.K., but outside the five mile limit, oh boy! It was lovely to pass up the Channel and see dear old England on the port side and all the horrors of this trip seemed to fade into the back of your memory, just as well. Past Dover we tramped, round the forelands and then made a beeline for the Thames and Tilbury. Safely tied up, over a glass of beer that evening, I reflected on the trip and decided that I would be very glad to get off this ship and let a bit of sanity return to my life for a short time. My time as a cadet was nearing its end and I would soon be going to college to sit my 2nd Mates ticket and be released from my contract with this shipping company and I had a strange feeling that once qualified I would not be returning to sail on their ships. But the only thing that I thought about at that moment of time was to walk down the gangway and go home.

I had Christmas at home and that to me was a real novelty. To have a nice tasty well cooked meal without worrying if the cook was going to have one of his turns or that one of the queer stewards thought that it was the wrong time of the month. To flop down in a chair with family and friends and not to worry about the green backs that you could see through the saloon porthole crashing over the bows and sweeping over No. 1 hatch and down the decks. It was nice to be home. New Years Day came and went and I wondered what 1962 had in store, but I did know that there was a lot of paperwork to face before I got my 2nd Mates.

On the 20th January I had a phone call from the company and they told me to go to Liverpool to be stand by crew for a few days whilst its Officers had a few days leave. I had to relieve the 3rd Mate and it made quite a change to hear all the moans and groans about the ship and the trip and to know that I only had a few days aboard before being able to get off it. There was a skeleton crew aboard and after a week all the cargo had been discharged and we moved out of the Mersey, myself acting as 3rd Mate and we took her up the west coast to Glasgow and into the dry dock. Glasgow was the shipping company's head office and I was summoned there for a meeting with my bosses. I was 19½ and too young to take my 2nd Mates as the youngest you could be was 20, another six months to go, but they released me from my apprenticeship and I walked out of the office a free person, it was over!

Yes it was over. In the past 3½ years I had seen places, done many things, had moaned a lot, and got soaked to the skin many times. But I had learnt a lot. Different people, different places, nice people, nasty people and, of course, the sea. I had seen it warm and inviting and the other side of it when it threw everything at you and tried to drown you. The shipping company, was it bad, had it all been a bad dream, I think not and on reflection I wouldn't have missed those years for the world. I often have a chat with people that were at sea about the same time as myself and as we talk about all the old shipping companies like Clan Line, Bibby Line, Elder Dempsters etc, they say "Do you remember that terrible shipping company that used to sail out of Greenock and what rust buckets they were?" and I say "Yes, I served my time with them", a look of respect comes into their eyes or is it sympathy?

PART TWO

Chapter 9

First Watch

I had got ahead of myself in life. It was February 1962 and I couldn't sit my 2nd Mates until August when I would then be 20 so it would have to be a spot of job hunting as I definitely couldn't stay on leave until then as my money was disappearing like water and I needed some finance behind me when I was at college. So after a few weeks leave I took the train up to London and went round some of the shipping offices to try and get a job as 4th Mate or uncertified 3rd Mate. After getting quite a few refusals I tried a company with a pretty good reputation and, bingo, they said yes. I was happy as they had a good fleet and many of their ships were on a regular run to South America, were modern vessels and carried twelve passengers. This was more like it I thought on the way back to Canterbury, at last I was to be an officer and a gentleman and have the young lady passengers swooning all over me as I stood on the bridge in my whites giving orders. I stayed on a high for a couple of days and when I got my orders to join my ship in Rotterdam I knew that I had got it wrong. The ship I was to join was built in 1942, which made it as old as me, and it wasn't a passenger ship and it wasn't South America, but the bloody North Atlantic again. Oh well, I thought, it can't be as bad as the last lot.

I got a late afternoon flight to Rotterdam and that night stayed at the Savoy Hotel where my new owners had booked me in so at least it was a step up as the last lot would have put me in the seamans home or some such place. After breakfast the next day I made my way up to the shipping agents offices to let them know that I had arrived and then took a taxi down to the docks to go aboard my new home. The ship on first view was what she was, old, but she looked well looked after and everything seemed to be pretty shipshape and tidy. I sought out the 3rd Mate's cabin and made myself known to the man I was going to relieve for the next trip. He was a nice chap and spent most of the morning showing me around and introducing me to my fellow officers and generally showing me the ropes. It all seemed a well run ship and my other shipmates seemed a good crowd and were all keen to help and advise me on any points that I needed to know. The 3rd Mate departed to return to England for his leave and I started to stow my gear away in my cabin, which was a novelty to me as it was the first time I didn't have to share my cabin with anyone else and I now had some privacy. The cabin was very spacious and it was not too badly painted out and I soon had it looking like home, or as close to it as circumstances allowed. So now I was the 3rd Mate aboard this ship and I had now to prove myself. I suppose that at 19 it was a pretty daunting task to have to be in charge of a 15,000 ton ship for so many hours a day on the bridge as well as peoples lives, but I was lucky and never worried too much about things and took things in my stride.

The ship was just about unloaded and the next day we would be moving into the dreaded dry dock for some engine repairs before then going to London to load a cargo for Canada. As 3rd Mate my position in the ship during entering and leaving harbour was on the bridge assisting the Captain or pilot and relaying orders to the helmsman, engine room when needed, the 1st Mate on the bows and the 2nd Mate down the stern. At least in this ship we had telephones to the bows and the stern so I didn't have to yell my guts out through a megaphone passing on orders. We moved into dry dock and spent two noisy, cold days there before moving out to a buoy to test the engine repairs and surprise, surprise we had more trouble with them and had to stay there an extra day while it was all sorted out. Things didn't change and I just hoped that the prop was okay on this ship. We eventually left Rotterdam at 19.30 and made our way down river towards the Hook and then on a heading towards the entrance of the Thames Estuary which wasn't a long trip. As 3rd Mate my watch was from 8-12 so by the time we got to the Hook it was time to go on watch and I was very glad in this instant that the Captain was on the bridge with me as it was my first watch and in this stretch of water there was a lot of shipping around, all coming from different directions and we had to do a lot of course alterations. It was an odd feeling to stand there and give the helmsman directions, port, starboard, steady as you go, with him repeating them and then the ship moving to its new heading. By now it was dark so all I could see was the white, red and green lights of the ships in our area and having to work out which way they were moving and if any danger to us, alter course to keep clear. Yes, I was very glad to have the Captain on the bridge that night to put me right and quietly telling me what to do and also to boost my confidence, also it started to get a bit rough with the wind coming up to a force 7. Those four hours seemed to fly by and suddenly the 2nd Mate was standing next to me ready to take over and stand his next four hours. I made a cup of tea in the chart room for myself, him and the Captain, who was still sitting in his chair in a corner of the dark bridge, then showed the 2nd the shipping that was in our vicinity and the ones that could be on a converging course, also the ships position on the chart. We chatted for about ten minutes, then saying goodnight to him and the Captain I left the bridge and made my way to my cabin and my lovely bunk. I was mentally worn out after those four hours, but quite content as I hadn't made too many balls ups and the ship was still afloat and with those thoughts floating round in my head I fell into a deep sleep.

After breakfast in the morning I was up on the bridge again at 08.00 to relive the 1st Mate and found that it was still blowing a gale with a blizzard thrown in for good measure. We had slowed down as we were to have picked up the Thames pilot, but he wouldn't have had a chance of getting on board in those conditions so we steamed around for a few hours until the weather abated. With the pilot on board eventually we started to move up the Thames and make our way to Tilbury and then to start loading our cargo of cars. By the time that we had got safely alongside the dockers only worked for an hour before they all sped off to their warm homes and the Captain, nice man that he was, said if I liked I could shoot off home for the night if I wished and as I had forgotten some books and other gear for my new position on the ship I was most grateful and was down the gangway like a scalded cat on the next train to Kent. After a pleasant night in my own bed at home I returned to the ship and was back on board by midday and by then the cars were being loaded fast and furiously and by 23.00 the pilot was aboard and we were saying goodbye to dear old London once again. For me this was a good hour to sail as it meant that I only had an hour on the bridge before I was off watch again.

When I got to the bridge the following morning we were heading down the Channel on a fine clear morning and not too much of a sea running. The Captain was there with the 1st Mate and they were talking about what jobs the bosun would be putting his men to. The Mate showed me the ships position and the ships that were around us then went off watch to enjoy his breakfast, with the Captain going down after about ten minutes and telling me that if I wanted any advice he would be in his cabin on the next deck down. I don't know who was the most nervous as he went below, him or I, and I had visions of him in his cabin peering out of the porthole to make sure that I was still on the right course or I wasn't running down some poor unsuspecting ship. So for the first time I was on the bridge by myself with the helmsman doing his job behind the wheel and me pacing up and down the bridge with a pair of binoculars slung around my neck trying to look at ease. The shipping around wasn't too bad as most of the vessels were moving up or down the Channel so there wasn't too much shipping crossing our course apart from the cross channel ferries that came at you like bats out of hell or the occasional fishing boats. Every half hour I took a fix on old England and marked the ships position on the chart as we plodded down the Channel and after a couple of hours I started to relax and even enjoy myself. I altered course a couple of times as I thought that we were getting a bit too close to another vessel for comfort, but on reflection I think that they must have been miles off and I was over cautious, but as the old man said later that it was better to be like that than to take chances. Time went past very quickly and before I knew it the 2nd Mate was standing next to me to take over again and that my first watch keeping period had ended.

So westward again, pointing our bows into the Atlantic once more, with me standing my watches from 8-12 each morning and evening and getting more used to my new found position. Once clear of the Channel we put the ship on the iron mike so this relieved the helmsman of standing there getting bored and for any course alterations I could do it. Apart from being on the bridge my other duties included checking the lifeboats were okay, also checking the fire fighting equipment on the ship, as well as keeping up with my studies. At least my navigation was improving as each day I had to work out the noon position with the 2nd Mate and by now I was pretty good at it, also I enjoyed it very much. Of course the engines had to play up and one day we were stopped for four hours, rolling all over the place as a cargo of cars didn't weight too much so we were quite high out of the water and with a beam on sea it wasn't too stable. The iron mike also broke down a few times so a moaning seaman had to take the helm while the engineers did their thing. The weather on that crossing was bad with very strong gales and one day we nearly lost the bosun over the side as he was working on the foredeck when we took a huge wave over the bows and the sea surged along the deck and took the bosuns legs from under him and he finished up in the scuppers hanging on for dear life. He was a very lucky man. A day out from Halifax, Nova Scotia, the port that we were heading for, we ran into pancake ice and for the next few hours had to crunch our way through that as well as being in a force 9 and a blizzard blowing. It wasn't too much fun standing a watch in those conditions, with both of the wheelhouse windows tightly shut to try and keep some warmth in the wheelhouse and either peering into the radar for long periods of time or trying to see out of the Kent clear view screen to see if there was any other ships mad enough to be out in these conditions. At least I was spared the job as lookout, stuck on the wing of the bridge trying to see ahead whilst trying to keep warm and stop the spray that came over the dodgers running down your collar. Some poor seaman had this job, or it was one of the ships cadets that had this privilege. Looking at them out there I counted my blessings.

We got to Halifax in the afternoon and as it was still snowing heavily no cargo was discharged for the rest of the day. I had a walk up town to have a look around, but the conditions were pretty bad so I didn't stay long and returned to my warm cabin. I had a drink with the chief steward when I got back and the customs officers was still with him helping to get rid of a bottle of Malt Whisky, so I joined in. An hour later the customs man said that he had better get going home and invited me and the steward to go home with him to have a meal and meet the family. We piled into his car and after a hairy drive we got to his home and had a very pleasant evening with him and his wife and children. Although most of the houses were made of wood out there they certainly know how to insulate them against the terrible weather conditions they have out in that part of the world and I'm sure they could teach us a thing or two in that field. About midnight we poured ourselves into a taxi and thanked our new friends for their hospitality and returned to our ship to collapse into our bunks, feeling well fed and watered, or Scotched. When we got up the following morning, with a large hangover, it had stopped snowing so off came the hatch covers and our cars started to be hoisted out of the depths of our holds and swung on to the snow covered quayside to be driven off to their departure point. As we only had to discharge about half of our cargo by 16.30 we had let go our ropes and were heading out into the fog that had by now shrouded everywhere. From here we were to make our way to Saint John, New Brunswick, about 300 miles and this trip took us around Cape Sable, the southern point of Nova Scotia, then up into the Bay of Fundy which was between the mainland and Nova Scotia. The trip round was evil with gales and blizzards all the time and I think that all on board were glad to get alongside and safely tied up. That night I stayed aboard as it was cold and still snowing so it was just as well to stay in a fairly warm cabin and not have to trudge up the road just for a drink. This was another fast turn around and by 16.00 the following day our holds were empty and we were ready to set sail again. So off into the vile weather we tramped again, this time we were making first for Quebec and then on to Montreal to load yet another cargo of grain for home. The distance to Quebec was about 1,300 miles and our course took us back round the bottom and then up the eastern coast of Nova Scotia before turning into the Cabot Strait, with Newfoundland on our starboard side then entering the Gulf of St. Lawrence. From here we went through the Gaspe Passage, with the large island of Anticosti to starboard before entering the large mouth of the St. Lawrence river. We picked up the river pilot and he had quite a long job to do as it's about 300 miles up to Quebec, with the river slowly getting narrower as we made our way up stream.

We got alongside about midday and as work wasn't going to start until the next day we got a chance to have a good look around and wonder of wonders the weather had improved and it was even quite warm. It really is a beautiful place with many old buildings and the whole place is steeped in history. Myself and my shipmates who were with me made our way up to the top of the heights where General Woolfe had done his thing against the French all those years ago. From up there the view was magnificent and you had a lovely view across the river and to the surrounding countryside. Well worth the long walk up there. I don't think the French ever forgave Woolfe for what he did to them and I found the locals very anti-English and they would speak in French if you asked them anything, even though most of them spoke English and they weren't very nice to us at all. So what's new! That night we had a very pleasant meal ashore in an English speaking restaurant and then went on to a couple of night clubs to see what the local girls were like, but once again they were not 100% for good looking English men. At least we had had a good look around and a good meal.

The next day they started to pour our grain into our holds and as we were only going to take on half cargo here by evening we were on the move once more. It seemed odd to me that we were going to finish off loading further upstream than Quebec rather than half a load at Montreal and then fill up at Quebec. I suppose that there must have been a reason, but I never found out. From Quebec to Montreal is only about 160 miles so not a long trip and as it was mainly night travel we didn't see a lot, but on the way back we had a good view of the countryside and it made an interesting voyage. We didn't get a chance to get ashore in Montreal, but it did look a very busy place with a lot of industry and a very large harbour. So with our holds full again we turned around and started on our 460 mile river trip before heading for dear old England. We dropped off our pilot and made our way across the Gulf again and then through the Cabot Strait to the North Atlantic. Back to watch keeping, but it was nice to get back into some form of routine and not having to dock every few days. The North Atlantic as usual at this time of the year wasn't kind to us, but on the few days it did settle enough to let some of the crew get on to the foredeck to do the endless painting of the ship, I looked down from the bridge and thought, ah yes, I used to do that. By now I was pretty relaxed on the bridge standing my watches and as there isn't too much shipping around in the middle of the Atlantic, it all became a bit boring at times. As we started to approach Ireland a few ships would start to appear and a few times I had to alter course for them, but I was starting to feel fairly confident in my ship handling, I'm sure to the relief of the whole ship's company.

Lands End and then the trip up the Channel, the busiest strip of water in the world, so this made me keep on my toes as most of the shipping was going with us or in the opposite direction, but it was the crossing vessels that I had to look out for, especially the cross channel ferries which charged across our bows at a great rate of knots, trying to keep to their time tables. Water taxis really. We picked up the Thames pilot and made our way once more to London to get rid of our grain and me, to have a few days leave. I had decided to do one more trip before going off to college and sitting my 2nd Mates, but before sailing off again I was going home for a few days peace and quiet. So my first trip as 3rd Mate was over and I was quite pleased with myself as I hadn't sunk the ship, or any other, not too many balls ups, and I must admit that apart from the terrible weather, I had enjoyed it.

Chapter 10

The Great Lakes

I knew that I was going to do one more trip before college, but this turned out to be two trip rolled into one and in total it lasted six months, a lot longer than I had reckoned on. On this trip we were to be going up to the Great Lakes and then returning back to the U.K. to discharge, but as we were getting close to Lands End on our voyage back we got orders to go to the continent to unload and then return to the Lakes with another cargo. This threw my planning out, but I must say that it was a couple of very interesting trips and when we were at the far end of the Lakes, as far as we could go across America by water, the ship was 602 feet above sea level, 1,350 miles inland and would have passed through 95,000 square miles of water.

I had been home about eleven days when I got my orders to rejoin the same ship that I had been on during my last trip, so at least I knew her and when I got back on board I found that it was the same master and most of the same officers which was good news as we all got on very well and we made a pretty good team. The bosun and the carpenter had also rejoined and the rest of the crew were a new bunch from London which wasn't too bad as the crews from here were usually a mixed lot, but always seemed to be a not too bad lot. The cook was also the same man as the last voyage which pleased everyone as he produced some good meals and I found out that he had been on a couple of the company ships that carried passengers so his standard had to be high on those vessels. So all in all it was a fairly happy ship and it needed to be as the weeks that we were inland in America were very hard work as we hopped from port to port every few days.

We slipped out of Dagenham on a foggy evening and by the time we got to the Thames Estuary it was like a pea souper and we dropped anchor for about five hours until it cleared a bit. I hated fog at sea, as did most people, and to have that damn fog horn sounding out its deep boom every few minutes day and night just about sent you loopy. Once we had a bit of visibility we upped anchor and tramped across to Flushing to fill those fuel tanks again, with only a few hours stay before we were heading down the Channel again and another Atlantic crossing. The weather had taken a turn for the better as we went down the Channel and we were averaging 13 knots in a flat calm sea. I thought that this was pushing her a bit and true to form we had three breakdowns on our Atlantic crossing, much to the engineers disgust. Our first port of call was to be Quebec to unload part of our cargo of cars before steaming on to Montreal to finish off unloading and then entering our first lock on our journey inland. We stayed in Quebec for three days and as I had been ashore here on our last trip and wasn't too impressed with the place, or more so, the locals, I didn't venture ashore much, only for a couple of beers in the evening. After the allotted amount of cars had been safely taken out of the holds and swung ashore we left and headed up the St. Lawrence River again and made our way towards Montreal. Once again it was a short stay of only twenty four hours and as I was duty officer no shore leave or time to have a look around, so once again no time to explore. The next day we had our first attempt at entering the St. Lawrence seaway, the gateway to the Lakes, but it wasn't as easy as we thought. The locks proved to be a lot of work and very long hours as there was a lot of waiting to be done and it was all very frustrating and boring. What happens is that we approach a lock and tie up at a waiting jetty outside the lock and wait for ships coming down to move out of the lock, the ships at the head of the queue move in and every one moves up a place until eventually it's your time to enter the lock. So with ships coming down and ships going up it's a very long process and it all becomes very tedious and monotonous. Eventually it was our turn to enter the lock and we nearly made it apart from the fact that we missed our lock entrance by about 2 feet and ran into solid concrete, taking a big lump of the bows off the ship and then having to retire to an empty lay-by berth for two days whilst repairs were carried out to our damaged stem. So we sat there for a couple of days with nothing to do while the shore crew did their thing to the ships bows to make us sea worthy again. We were near a small village and in the afternoons we played the locals at football and in the evenings went up to the local bar to celebrate with them as they beat us at every game. After two days we were ready to have another go at entering the lock, with a different pilot and with the Captain having kittens we made another attempt at entering and this time we made it. Once tied up safely in the lock the gates closed behind us and the water started gushing in and we were on our way up. We got to the right height and the front gates opened and we moved slowly forward along the canal. It was all very nervy as the canal was very narrow and with ships coming towards you in that confined space it all took a lot of concentration, especially the helmsman as when a large ship approached you it took the water away from you and it made steering very hard as the ship swung all over the place. The seaway was about 26 miles long and it took us most of the day to get through, what with all the hanging around to enter the locks and by the time that we got clear we were then 326 feet above sea level with about the same height to go again. From the end of the seaway we went into our first lake, Ontario, which is the smallest of all the lakes and to me one of the deadest with water that looked foul and I doubt that anything at all lived in there. From the seaway it was about 170 miles to our first port of call, Toronto, where we would start the long process of loading with many stops on the way. This is where I first saw the local type of boat called the Laker which trades between all the ports in the lakes and carries cargo from port to port all within the Great Lakes. They are long low boats with a wide beam and I didn't fancy being on them as to me there was an awful lot of work involved going from port to port with a lot of locks in between. We arrived at Toronto at 14.30 and loading started straight away and by 23.00 we had the hatch covers on and we were ready to sail first thing in the morning.

I didn't get ashore here as the 2nd Mate had relations living here and the Captain let him ashore to go visiting when we docked so once again I was duty officer. It was an early morning start the following day and by 05.00 we were on our way and steaming the 40 miles to the entrance to the Welland canal and some more locks. The distance we had to go through the canal and the locks was 21 miles and believe it or not it took us till midnight to clear this stretch of water. Gone was all the nice steady routine of watch keeping and on that day I was on the bridge from 05.00 until midnight as were the 1st Mate and his crowd stuck at the bows and the 2nd Mate at the stern of the ship. It was a very long and boring day and everyone aboard was glad when we eventually got clear of the canal and entered Lake Erie. Lake Erie was the shallowest of all the lakes and as we made our way on the next 240 miles to Toledo it looked just as polluted and as dead as the last one we had passed through. Each lake had a pilot to navigate us through and on this trip we had a very nice man called Mr. Burke who lived in Cleveland and he helped to pass the time on my watch by us having long conversations and I learnt a lot about the American way of life through him.

We arrived at Toledo and once again it was to be a fast turnaround with our cargo being winched into the holds and within twenty four hours we were ready to move on again. I must say that I wasn't worried about not getting ashore here as it seemed to be a very large industrial city, but as it was the capital of Ohio it was a thriving city. It had a large natural harbour and there was a lot of shipping movements all the time with the large lakers coming and going at all hours. In went more cargo, on went the hatches again and off we went again, travelling the 50 miles up the coast to Detroit, which stands on the western end of Lake Erie and also on the banks of a place called Lake St. Clair, which is land locked between Erie and Huron. Detroit is a massive city with a population of about 1 million people, the home of the Ford motor car and a murder rate of about nine hundred per year! We stayed overnight there and a few of us made our way up to the city centre for a few beers, but we got a taxi there and back as we didn't think that it was the place to wander round late as night and we didn't want to be murder victim number nine hundred and one.

By now the crew were getting really fed up with the hours that had to be worked and it was only with a lot of tact that the 1st Mate stopped a strike, but even then one of the crew jumped ship in Detroit and that was the last we saw of him. All of us weren't too impressed with the hours we had to work and the amount of ports that we were stopping off at, but we all had to just get on with the job. At least we only had a few more ports to load before we headed back east again, but even then we had to go through all those damn locks again.

From Detroit we were next going into Lake Huron, but first locks and another canal. Once we got into Huron at least we were going to be at sea, or lake, for a few days as our next port was to be Chicago, a distance of about 650 miles which took us up to the top of Lake Huron through the strait of Mackinac and then down to the bottom of Lake Michigan, which is the only lake that is totally in the United States. It is also the third largest of the lakes with an area of about 62,000 square kilometres, a lot of water. On the way down we encountered some pretty rough weather conditions and it surprised us just how bad it could become, with strange seas, not like the type one finds in the open ocean. We arrived at Chicago on a Sunday morning so at least some of us had the day off to have a look around this gigantic city. It is a vast place with lots of industry and it is called the economic centre of the mid west and in the centre of the city it is a maze of towering office blocks stretching up to the sky. Chicago's population in those days was about 3 million so it gives you some idea of just how large the place is and it then boasted of having the largest airport in the world. In the evening the 2nd Mate and myself had a pleasant meal ashore and then decided to take a trip down to Harlem and visit some of the night clubs. On reflection I suppose that it was a stupid thing to do as in most of the clubs we were the only white folk there and in a couple of dimly lit joints all we could see were white teeth and white eyes and everything else was black! The atmosphere was great down there and at about 2 o'clock in the morning I had the best pizza of my life there, served by an enormous black man from a mobile cafe in the street. The local people treated us well and made us welcome, but after we staggered back to the ship the local night watchman said that we were lucky not to have been mugged and had our throats cut.

Work started first thing the next morning and by the end of the day we had our assortment of cargo in our holds and we left for the next leg of our trip. Back up the lake again with the state of Wisconsin to port and Michigan to starboard and we were making for the Sault St. Marie locks and the Soo Canal which would then take us into the last of the lakes, Superior. We would then be 602 feet above sea level. We would be calling at two ports in this lake, Port Arthur which is Canada, and then down a few miles to Duluth which is in the States and is the furthest you can go inland in the lakes. Lake Superior, as its name suggests, is the largest of all the lakes and, in fact, is the largest sheet of fresh water in the world with the grand area of about

115

83,000 square kilometres of the stuff. From the Soo Canal to Port Arthur was about 250 miles and we encountered some vile weather on the way and after we passed Isle Royal, a nature reserve, we had to anchor up for quite a few hours in a place called Thunder Bay, which was just off Port Arthur, to let the weather calm down a bit before we could enter port. Eventually the wind abated and our pilot decided to take us in and once again we were safely tied up alongside. We worked cargo until about 17.00 then a few of us gave the local dockers a game of football before going uptown to have a meal then an evening at the local cinema. The next day off came the hatches and in went the cargo and by now this was driving the 1st Mate and 2nd Mate mad as we were loading general cargo, but having to leave space in the lower holds to pick up bulk grain at Montreal on the way back, so to keep the stability of the ship right it was proving a nightmare to them. By the end of the day we were on the move again, but the end was in sight as Duluth was to be our last port, much to the relief of all aboard. So we travelled the 170 miles down the coast passing once more from Canada to America and this was only an fourteen hour passage. By now everyone on board from the Captain down was fed up with all this hopping from port to port and we would all be grateful when we could point our bows eastward once more and head for open waters and get back to some form of routine. So down the coast we headed crossing from Canada to America once again, but at least the last port of call was soon to be in sight. We didn't actually dock in Duluth, but a smaller place on the outskirts called Superior which seemed like a nice area. We stayed here for five days whilst the rest of the cargo was loaded, leaving the lower holds clear for the grain we would be picking up at Montreal. After the first day I had to take to my bunk for the next four days as I got a touch of the dreaded malaria again and I felt pretty grim. the doctor from the town came to see me and gave me some medicine and pills which seemed to do the trick and I managed to take a walk up to the town on the last day to have a haircut and have a look around. It looked a very pleasant little place and the locals made me feel at home and were very hospitable.

And it came to pass on the fifth day that the ship was ready to turn round and make her way through the largest expanse of fresh water in the world and head for the open seas. Even the crew cheered up and the talk of strikes receded. Our ropes were let go and we left the furthest point in the lakes and started the long arduous trip back the way we had come, but at least our first port was to be Montreal. Superior, Huron, Erie, Ontario, many hours of tying up, moving along the lay-by berth, entering locks, dropping down in feet above sea level, passing along canals until at last we came to the St. Lawrence Seaway, the final part of this inland passage. But life doesn't run a smooth passage and as we were moving along a narrow part of a canal a large laker came very close to us in the opposite direction, taking water from us and giving us no steerage way. We hit this bridge pretty hard and once again our poor bows had a big hole put in them. They say lightning doesn't strike twice, but I'm not too sure about that. We only had one more lock to clear before we got out of the seaway and when we cleared this the pilot took us, once again, to a lay-by berth where we stayed for two days while the front of the ship was made seaworthy. After the bows were repaired we moved over to the gain silo and our bulk cargo was poured into the holds. From Montreal back to Montreal had taken twenty eight days of hard work, long hours and tight ship handling and we all breathed a sigh of relief as the ropes were let go and we started to wend our way back down the St. Lawrence river and to open waters. For the next eleven days we could all settle down to the usual routine and back to the mundane jobs of every day ship life. The crossing back across the Atlantic wasn't too bad with varying weather and as we

117

approached Lands End we all got chatting about what we would be doing this time next week when we would be on leave. The radio officer appeared on the bridge with a long face and handed a radio message to the Captain. The ship was not going to London, but to Rotterdam to unload, then move round the continental ports loading general cargo before returning back up the lakes. Once we had got tied up in Rotterdam the crew signed off and fled back to England as fast as they could, not wanting to have another easy cruise up the lakes. A new crew were sent out to us, not knowing where the ship would be making for. Most of the officers had to stay, but some of the lucky ones were transferred to other ships in the company, some went home for a few days leave while the ship moved round the continent. I had to stay for another trip and in all it was to be six months from the time of joining until I set foot on English soil again. At least I was getting some good experience as 3rd Mate and this would help when I came to sit my exams also I was saving some money for my time ashore.

I left the ship on 1st September 1962 and started at King Edward VII College three weeks later.

Chapter 11

Russians and Risor

I spent the next five months ashore in London at the King Edward VII College studying and sitting my 2nd Mates ticket. It was just like being back at school , but we were all big boys and all of a kindred spirit and we used to play hard as well as work hard. Of course all my class mates were all seamen, some with big passenger companies, some with tankers and some like myself with good old fashion tramping companies, in fact a cross section of all maritime shipping. When we first met and told each other whom we had been cadets with a look of pity crossed my friends faces as I explained with which company I had spent the last four years, also a look of respect. The lads that had served their time with the larger companies had been treated as officers and gentlemen and spent most of their apprenticeship on the bridge of the ships that they had been on and didn't know the joys of bilge diving or trying to paint the top of the mast as the ship rolled all over the place, but at least I had one advantage over them, I knew how to do it. If in the exams there were questions on bilges at least I would know the answers. College was from 9am to 5pm and in that time we had to absorb a lot of information over a wide range of subjects and even then we had a lot of homework to do in the evenings. Apart from the theoretical part we also had to do a lot of practical subjects such as doing a two day fire fighting course at the local fire station. This was fun and we had to do things like crawling through a smoke filled tunnel with breathing apparatus on dragging a straw filled sack that was supposed to have been a body. Also we had to do a radar course which involved a lot of theory, but also it included going up and down the Thames in a large launch which was fitted out with a lot of radar sets that we had to get used to and have to set up. This was a lot of fun and as I had used the radar a lot when I was sailing as 3rd Mate on the last two trips it was all a bit of a holiday for me and I enjoyed the days out on the Thames. First aid was another course we had to do and it always baffled me that as soon as the lecturer started to talk about broken bones and fractures there would be a crash and one of the lads would have passed out and finished up on the floor. God knows what would have happened when it came to the real thing. So the courses went on with a multitude of different subjects such as signals, ship construction, navigation, principles of navigation (a real nasty subject), buoyage, rules of the road, maths, electricity and many, many more. We all worked hard and we all played hard and the local nurses home was one of the local favourite spots, so much so that I even got engaged to a lovely nurse for a few months, but got disengaged when I returned back to sea much to her regret. We had some wild parties and one night I finished up with two Swedish girls back at their flat and when I eventually arose I realised I was an hour late for college. When I entered the lecture room and was asked why I was late I said that I was trying to improve Swedish/English relationships much to the amusement of my mates, but not of the lecturer.

During my stay in London I was lucky enough to have board and lodgings with friends of my parents, a lovely couple called Henry and Wynn, who had a very large house at Tulse Hill and they treated me like a son. Henry had a wonderful job in the docks which involved looking after an empty warehouse of which he had been doing for years. This involved going down to the docks every day to make sure that nothing had been stolen, which was pretty unlikely as it was empty, then he got down to the real hard work which was reading and cleaning his car and at the end of each week he would collect his pay packet. That is what I called a pressurised job. Wynn was a great lady and a true Londoner with a big sense of humour. I remember coming home one evening and I couldn't find her anywhere, but eventually I heard this moan from the cellar. I went down and found her legless and when I got her sober she said that she had decided to go and test Henry's home made wine of which she had mixed about six different types and drank about three bottles. No wonder she got stoned as it was powerful stuff and she said that she wouldn't let a drop more pass her lips. They were a smashing pair and I was very sad when I heard a few years later that they had passed on.

On a cold, wet February morning the time had arrived to take my exams and a group of nervous young men opened the first paper and tried to remember all that had been taught to us over the past four years. We waded our way through the papers until Thursday and on the Friday it was time for the dreaded oral exam. This involved being questioned for up to an hour by an examiner, usually a man with an extra masters ticket, on anything connected with the sea and shipping. You just hoped that the questions came up that you knew the answers to and didn't make too many cock ups. This was a real test of nerves, a bit like taking your driving test except a hundred times as bad, and many a pound in weight had been shed in that room as the sweat rolled off you. On the Friday night it was all over and apart from a few lads the rest of us passed so it was out for a celebratory drink, or to drown ones sorrows in the case of the poor blokes who had to do it all again. We all parted and went our different way, hoping either to meet up in about two years time when we would return to sit our 1st Mates ticket or meet up in some foreign port and have a few drinks together.

My time at college was over and after a couple of weeks leave it was back to getting a job. I gave the shipping company that I had last sailed with a phone call and they said that they had an interesting little job for me before putting me back to sea. It turned out that the company had just sold one of their older ships and it was in dry dock in London waiting for the new buyers to turn up and make sure that all was well aboard and up to the standard they required. My job was to help in the takeover and show the new crew around and help as much as I could to make it all go smoothly. Out of interest I asked who was buying the ship and the man at the other end of the phone gave a little chuckle and said "The Russians". This was going to be interesting. So I packed my bags and made my way up to London by train and got a taxi to the Red Ensign Club where the company had booked me in for my stay in town. I found out that the twenty or so Russians I was soon to meet were also booked in there and I thought it rather apt that they were staying at a place that flew a red flag over the main door! I got settled in and the next day made my way down to the dry dock and went aboard the old ship that would soon be flying the hammer and sickle. The head docker introduced me to the head Russian and he looked as though he had just stepped out of a James Bond spy film with a long black coat that went down to the floor and a hat that covered most of his face. He was the head man, the commissar, the powerful one who the rest held in awe. He was also a right sod and nearly caused a strike more than once as he followed the dockers round as they did their jobs and he would say "not good enough". The head docker had to use all his skills as a negotiator with the dockers as they weren't too impressed with the man in the dark coat. As some of the ship was being painted he would check that they hadn't missed a bit and if they had it was straight to the supervisor to complain. The rest of the Russians were the officers and crew who would be taking the ship out of the dry dock and sailing her away to the motherland. They were okay and the same as any seamen anywhere in the world and were basic down to earth men. I got to know them well as we were all staying at the same place and I had long chats with them in the evenings as they explained about their homeland and their families and they all seemed to have the same hopes and worries as any of us. They loved to show me photographs of their families back home and I still have some postcards that they gave me as keepsakes. The ones that have tanks on I'm not too impressed with! One evening after dinner I mentioned to one of them that I was going to the cinema and he asked if he could come with me and me being me said of course. I don't suppose that many people can say that they took twenty Russians to see a film, but that's what I finished up with and it was quite a hoot to get them all on a London bus and take them up town and usher them into the cinema while the usherette gave me a most peculiar look. I don't know if they understood the film, but they all seemed to enjoy themselves and couldn't thank me enough, that was of course everyone apart from the commissar who didn't come, but took notes when we all got back and gave me some filthy looks. It made we wonder if I was on a hit list.

It took just over a week before the ship was handed over and they were more or less happy with her. I know that one problem arose and that was that the company couldn't find the keys to the safe in the Captains cabin and as it contained some drugs and a revolver it had to be opened. I mentioned this to the head docker and he said not to worry and sent one of his side kicks to find this small weasel type man. He came up to the Captains cabin and had a look at the safe and said no trouble at all and asked us all to step outside for a few minutes and shut the door behind him. About three minutes later he opened the door to let us in and showed us the open safe with the gun, some papers and the drugs inside. We didn't ask him how he did it, money changed hands and everyone was happy and I didn't even ask him what he did in the evenings and at weekends! The Russian crew took over and the dry dock was flooded and they moved out with the pilot taking them down to the entrance to the Thames before they put the ships bows in the direction of Russia and back to their homes. It had all been an experience and it was nice to know that Russian seamen are the same as us with the same problems in life. It was time for a few more days at home before joining my next ship and getting back to sea as it seemed like a long time since I had smelt the open waters.

After a few days relaxing at home I gave the company a ring to see what jobs they had to offer me. British & Commonwealth were a very large organisation and had a lot of shipping companies under their umbrella and so when they said they needed a 3rd Mate for one of their Bowater ships I was more than pleased as these were smart well run vessels and had a good reputation. The other good factor was that the run was to be from Ridham docks, which were in Kent so only a few miles from home, to Risor in Norway which was only a stones throw away. I felt that life was on the up as I made the short train journey from home to Ridham and I was looking forward to feeling a ships deck under me again. As the taxi I got from the station got closer to the docks I saw my future home quite a way off as the Bowater house mark on the yellow funnel stood out well and I had seen their ships whilst I had been tramping and had always thought what nice ships they were and envied the people aboard, but still now it was my turn. She was about 6,481 gross tons with a length of 419 feet and a beam of 59 feet and according to my findings had a turn of speed of just on 14 knots. As I went on board I could see that she was a well maintained ship, everything well painted and all neat and Bristol fashion and my cabin, when I found it was, very comfortable with some nice furniture and it all looked nice and cosy, sort of home from home. I made myself known to the Captain and then introduced myself to the other mates who were on board and they all made me very welcome and said if I needed to know anything, just ask. The ship had just arrived back from its trip from Norway so we still had quite a bit of paper pulp to unload before returning to Risor to pick up some more paper. I didn't bother to go ashore in the evenings whilst we were there as the ship was very comfortable and apart from that I was having a passionate affair with this woman back home and she didn't mind driving up to the ship each night to give my bunk an inspection before returning home in the early hours of the morning, so everything I needed was aboard. Happy days! The food was excellent and the crew were a very good bunch as well they might be as the trips were short and they could tell their families nearly to the hour when they would be home so it all made for a happy ship. The bridge was well equipped and it even had a fridge tucked away in a corner in case you got hungry on watch and this was a luxury I hadn't encountered before. As the cargo was paper pulp the ship was kept clean, not like the good old days of coal or sulphur covering the whole ship.

So after a few days that were fairly easy and some hard nights we were ready to wind our way down the Thames and make for the open waters on our short crossing to Norway, which was about 650 miles and take us near on thirty six hours. Once clear of the Thames Estuary we headed in a north easterly direction making for the Naze which is the southern tip of Norway before entering the Skagerrak and then travelling up the eastern coast of Norway a few miles to Risor. The crossing was rough as the North Sea in March isn't the best place in the world to be at that time of the year and as we were a light ship we were buffeted all over the show and rolled like a drunken sailor. When we entered the Skagerrak and moved up the coast of Norway, the scenery was spectacular with high hills verging on mountains and the whole sight was breath taking. When we got to Risor all that was there was a large paper mill and a long jetty to which we tied up to. I asked where the town was and was informed that it was over the very high hill that overshadowed us. It was all very peaceful and the scenery that surrounded us was once again a joy to look at and very mountainous and beautiful. We were to be there about five days loading so it gave me a chance to get my bearings and have a look around the small town that lay the other side of the hill. It was a long hard slog to get there and after walking up the very steep hill and down the other side I wondered it if was all worth it. When you got there the town was a bit of a disappointment as there wasn't much on offer and what with the prices that were well beyond our reach and the very strict laws on the sale of alcohol and drinking, I didn't stay too long in that sleepy little town. There was one place that a few of the seamen took advantage of and that was a house on the top of the hill we had to climb to get into town and this was run by a few ladies that offered relief to any one interested, at a price. I was led to believe that it was originally run by women that were collaborators during the Second World War and that they had been made outcasts by the town so they had set up their business at the top of the hill. I supposed that it had been handed down to the next generation and was still running, just like a family business. I never ventured in, but was told that the service was pretty good! After a couple of visits to town I didn't bother much after that and saved my money for back at home.

So the ship was slowly filled up with the large heavy bales of paper pulp and once we were loaded down to the plimsoll line we turned our bows around and started on the short trip back to the U.K. Most of the time that we were in Ridham I stayed aboard and didn't go dashing off home for a few days leave as the ship was comfortable, the food good, and my rampant lady still didn't mind driving up to the ship when we were there. Life was good and I hoped to stay on this ship and run for some considerable time, but life isn't like that and as I have said in a previous chapter that after a few trips I got struck down by the dreaded malaria again and finished up in the Gravesend isolation hospital, thus this nice ship and short trips came to an end, mores the pity. It was sad as she was a happy ship. After a few days leave after getting discharge from hospital I phoned the shipping company up and waited to see what ship would be next and to what part of the world I would be making for next.

Chapter 12

South America

When I received my orders to join my next ship I was more than happy and in fact stayed with this shipping company, sailing on a number of their ships as 3rd and 2nd Mate until I finished with my career at sea in 1964. The company I was to join was the South American Saint Line which had an excellent reputation and had fast modern ships and it was to be a regular run from London, about five continental ports, then down to north Spain, Lisbon, the Canary Isles then south to the eastern coast of South America calling at about six ports before heading back to England. This was a good run and kept to a fairly regular time table, apart from when the unexpected happened. The cargoes were to be general cargo out and then grain and general back and at times a few horses thrown in for good luck. Apart from the cargo the ships had another attraction and that was that they carried about twelve passengers and this made life interesting. As officers we had the task of organising entertainment for them and keeping them amused which at times wasn't so amusing for us. As we carried passengers the ships had to be of a high standard so the ships were kept in good condition and the food aboard them was fit for a king and on reflection I will never know how I managed to consume so much and still stay slim. The passengers enjoyed their time with us, some doing the round trip, some going out to South America to work, some returning back home after a stint out there. It passed the time talking to them and most were good company apart from a few of the blue rinse brigade who could at times be a pest. Once we got clear of the Canary Isles and started on our trip down to South America we would construct a swimming pool on top of No. 3 hatch which was just below the bridge and it was fun to watch the ladies in their bikinis splashing around in the water giving me the glad eye as I peered over the wing of the bridge. Some of the sights were horrendous as those overweight ladies flopped around like grounded whales thinking that they were Esta Williams. Once we got into the warmer climates it had a strange effect on the women and they suddenly became very amorous and it wasn't funny being cornered by some middle aged woman who wanted your attention so a lot of tact had to be used before making your escape to the safety of your cabin. Most passengers were very nice, but now and then an awkward one sailed with us, but was soon put in their place. I remember, and well I might, very well we had to take twelve nurses down to Buenos Aires and they weren't male nurses, but young red blooded females. This was a fun trip and the Captain went mad on his Sunday inspection as when he got down to the crews accommodation he would find a bra or a slip that weren't on the owner, but hung up to dry or draped over the back of a chair. He would give the senior nurse a good talking to, but as she was as rampant as her charges it was like talking to a brick wall so in the end the Captain gave up and everyone enjoyed the trip. Happy memories! As we carried passengers the officers had to look smart and watch their language so at times we had to bite our tongues. A lot of the stewards aboard were as queer as clockwork oranges and the passengers loved them as they were very good at their jobs and also entertaining. I had a steward to do my washing, cleaning and keeping my cabin clean and he/she was nicknamed Maggie the Snatch. He looked after me like a mother and my uniform was always spotless and beautifully ironed, as was my cabin which was kept spotless. It was always hilarious to watch the stewards dressed up in their best dresses or frocks, high heels on, faces all made up, tripping down the gangway in some foreign port to go and meet some of their so called sisters or cousins.

Still, they were very good at their jobs and each to their own I say.

The ships were about 7,000 gross tons with an average speed of 15 knots and they looked very sleek and modern and during my stay with them they didn't break down too often. Most of the officers and crew had been with the shipping company for some time as they seemed to know which side their bread was buttered. Quite a few of the officers had married girls from South America and brought them back to England to live so when we were down there they had to visit families and relations of the wives. I never could work out if this was a good or bad thing as they had to behave themselves when they went ashore. My fellow officers were all a great lot and we had a great deal of fun aboard and ashore and I considered these very happy ships with a lovely atmosphere.

As I have said the cargoes that we picked up around the continent was mainly general, no bulk, and it was quite a headache to work out a loading plan as goods were being discharged as we were loading at the same time and it was a job to make sure that the ship was stable at all times. On the South American coast we would pick up a few tons of bananas to ship them on to another port and this wasn't a great deal of fun as out of the pallets of bananas would crawl all these nasty big spiders, snakes and other creepy crawlies. I don't know about the others aboard, but I know that I gave my bunk a good inspection before getting into it just to make sure that it hadn't become a home to one of these unwelcome seafarers. On the way back to the U.K. we would stop at the Canary Isles to pick up pallets of tomatoes when they were in season, which if I recall was most of the time. The main cargo we shipped home was bulk grain in the lower holds and in the tween decks corned beef, hides, hoof and horn, bone meal and a few other odds and sods. On a couple of trips we had stables constructed on the main deck and we shipped polo ponies which are about the best in the world and as the Captain knew that I did a lot of riding and looking after horses when I was on leave it fell on my shoulders to take care of them. I didn't mind at all so each day it was mucking out, water and feed them also I gave them a groom to keep them in good condition. It always surprised me how well they travelled and even in a strong gale they did pretty well. On one trip I had to look after about ten Fallabella's, the smallest horse in the world, and these stood about the same height as a Great Dane and were all put into one large stable. They were great fun to look after and I became very attached to them each with their own personalities, most very well behaved, but a pair of right little sods amongst them. On arrival back in London the owner came down to see if they were all okay as they were pretty valuable, and when he saw the condition of them he was well pleased and so was I when he gave me a fat cheque for looking after them so well. When I finished my career at sea I went into the horse world and with my contacts in the Argentine I imported horses back to England to train them as show jumpers, polo ponies, eventers and hunters, but that is another story!

Tilbury, this is where the trip started and ended so the passengers came aboard here whilst we were unloading and loading our cargo ready for the next trip. From here we set out on our continental trek, calling at Antwerp, Bremen, Bremenharven, Hamburg and usually a couple more thrown in for good luck as we spent the next seventeen days hauling cargo out of the holds and putting more in. In Antwerp I had become friendly with one of the shipping agents and one Saturday night I and one of the other mates was round his house having a drink with him and his wife when he asked us if we liked cricket. Yes, we both said out of politeness, only to find the next day we were playing for his cricket side, somewhere in Holland. Of course we got thrashed, but it was a nice day out and we did see a bit more of

131

Holland than we usually did. We didn't get asked to play again as we both got ducks and I worked it out that it can't be a very popular sport over there if they had to go down to the docks to get a team together.

It was along this coast line that I came the closest to causing a collision and scaring myself half to death in the process. In one part of the sea in that area it was tight navigation and we had to steer from buoy to buoy along a restricted channel with about half a mile each side of the buoys to keep within. I was sailing as 2nd Mate on this trip and was enjoying having the bridge to myself during the afternoon as the old man had gone below to have a snooze so I just had the helmsman on the bridge with me as we picked our way from buoy to buoy. I noticed off the port bow a small coaster that was crossing the main shipping lane and that if it didn't alter course it would be on a collision course. As it got closer and closer and didn't change course as it was supposed to have done, laid down by the rules of the road at sea, I started to get a bit panicky as coming down towards us was a lot of shipping and I couldn't turn to starboard to get clear of the fast approaching coaster. When it was inevitable there was going to be a collision I told the helmsman to go hard a port and I ran to the ships whistle and started to sound the ships horn. Now if the other ship had done the correct thing he would have turned to starboard and we would have collided. The Captain came to the bridge at a run as soon as he heard the whistle and by then we were half way round our turning circle and my nerves were shot to hell. When we had got back on our true course the Captain and I had a close look at the offending vessel through the binoculars and could see no one on the bridge at all so we assumed that the ship must have been on automatic pilot and that everyone was below having a cup of tea or something and unaware of how close they had come to having a collision and possibly losing their lives. At times like that you realise that some people shouldn't be allowed to go to sea and put lives in danger. It had shaken me up that incident, but the Captain was very understanding and what he called the other ships Captain and officers I couldn't print it. When you think that the channel and waters around there have about 36,000 ships a year passing through it and that doesn't count for the cross channel vessels and you get some fool like that not keeping a proper watch it makes you wonder that there aren't more accidents at sea.

The two to three weeks round the continent was hard work for us as we were in and out of port like yo-yo's with cargo doing the same. We didn't get much time ashore there, but I did manage to go ashore in Hamburg a few times to see what the night life offered and that was quite an eye opener. Each night over dinner in the saloon the passengers would tell us all the exciting things that they had seen and done and at times it was hard to work up enthusiasm as most of us had done it or been there, but it was part of our job to keep them happy and that is what we did, bless them. I think that all the working people on the ship gave a sigh of relief when at last we had picked up our quota of cargo and were ready to slip out into the channel and make our way south. It was nice to be back in open waters again and although it only took about six days to get to Lisbon life set back into a routine once more. As the ship was nearly loaded down to her plimsoll line we sat well in the water so it didn't roll around too much and this pleased the passengers as a lot of them hadn't been to sea before and didn't quite know what to expect. I know that a few times when we crossed Biscay and the weather wasn't at its kindest, with a force 9 gale blowing, the saloon in the evenings wasn't too busy and a lot of the passengers took to their bunks and didn't feel too good and wondered if they had made the right decision to come on a cruise. Once the weather had abated and they all felt well again I am sure that they wrote home saying how they had survived a hurricane and that it hadn't effected them. Human nature I suppose.

The trip up the River Tagus to Lisbon was about 7 miles and I think that Kodak made lots of profit judging by the amount of photographs that were taken as we approached the huge bridge that spans the river, with the tall statue of Christ on the right hand side just before we arrived at Lisbon. This was a port that I enjoyed and had lots of fun ashore here as I think did most of the crew aboard. I got involved with a very pretty Portuguese girl who I took on to a few night clubs. At about midnight she asked me in her broken English if I would like to go back to her parents house to meet them and have a drink. Me, with my spattering of Spanish, agreed and when we got there they were still up and made me most welcome with a few bottles of wine and we all got on like a house on fire. At about 2 o'clock I said that I must return to the ship and get a few hours sleep. The father wouldn't hear of it and insisted that I stayed the night and pointed to a bedroom and told me I could sleep the night there. Being an officer and a gentleman I agreed and was pleasantly surprised to find out that it was also his daughters bedroom! I spent many happy nights at that house.

I liked Lisbon. The main problem for us on board was where the ship was moored as there was a terrific rise and fall of the tide and the current was very, very strong. We broke many wires and ropes there and at night we even had to have a seaman on watch to make sure that we remained tied up to the quay. I know that Lisbon had a beautiful harbour, but it did cause us a lot of headaches. After a couple of days our cargo was loaded and we were ready to move out back down the river and head our bows towards Las Palmas in the Canary Islands to pick up more fuel and water. It was only a two day trip and by then the weather usually had warmed up and the Captain told us to change into our whites and expose our knees to the sun and the passengers, so away went our blue uniforms for a few weeks. Our stay on our outward trip at Las Palmas was only a few hours and then we set off on our 3,000 mile trek making for Recife, or as it was called Pernambuca, which is situated on the most easterly point of north east South America, if that makes sense. The only land that we saw on the nine day crossing was the outline of the Cape Verde Islands with its volcanic mountains sticking out of the sea in the distance. The weather was good to us on this stretch of ocean, but it got very hot as we approached the equator and we were glad of the small breeze that the ship made as she motored through the sea. The passengers lounged around all day either sun bathing or taking advantage of the makeshift swimming pool and trying to keep cool. We organised games for them and tried to keep them amused as best we could and when we crossed the line we had a crossing the line ceremony which they all enjoyed and then we laid on a party for them which everyone enjoyed. The seas were flat and the skies blue with very little shipping around and the only thing that broke the monotony was the occasional school of whales that romped around us and this always caused a lot of excitement with the passengers. When we got to Recife the heat hit you like a tone of bricks once we had tied up and with little or no breeze we sweated buckets and it wasn't surprising that we drank so much to replace the lost body fluid. Recife lay about 500 miles south of the equator so it wasn't really surprising that it was so hot. It is called the Venice of Brazil because of its natural harbour and its peninsula state, but that was as far as it goes as the buildings ashore didn't really compare with Venice itself and it had a huge shanty town on the outskirts. It was quite an industrial place with a huge petro-chemical works that employed a lot of people, but to me it wasn't the place that I wanted to retire to and the heat after a few days really got you down. What I was surprised about was the different races that lived there and there was a very large Chinese population in the town as well as big communities of all races and creeds. Going ashore was very cheap with the cost of meals and drinks well within our reach and I loved the atmosphere and its pulsating music wherever you went and the locals made us more than welcome. The other thing about Brazil was that on every corner there was a crowd of boys or young men playing football and at most of the ports that we called at in this country at one stage or another we made up a team and gave one local team or another a game. God this was hard work in that heat and we played a shorter version than the usual match and at the end of an hour we had lost pounds in sweat and had to go to the nearest bar to replace the lost fluids. In those days Brazil was about the best football team in the world and I reckon that they must have been spoilt for choice with all the talent around. The Brazilian girls were beautiful with long black hair and lovely brown eyes and they seemed to like the English, which was very handy, as we liked them! We stayed at Recife for about two or three days and I think that all aboard were glad when we had discharged the cargo for there and could put back to sea and get a bit of a breeze as we made our way down the coast another 450 miles to Bahia which is the capital of the state of Salvador. This was quite a large port and its main exports are coffee, sugar, tobacco, oil and cocoa and on our homeward trip we called in here to pick up cargo for the U.K. or the continent, but southward we discharged some general cargo. Once again it is a large city and quite industrial with some very large factories and a huge population. It wasn't my favourite port of call, but there again they can't all be good. After the allotted amount of cargo departed our holds back to sea and another 800 miles to Rio. It was on one trip on this part of our voyage that I got promoted to 2nd Mate and I must have proved myself as on future trips I kept that rank. This was all due to the Chief Officer on this trip who went mad! We were a couple of days from Rio when he lost his marbles and started to creep around the ship at night with a fire nozzle in his hand trying to hit us over the head. This wasn't funny and standing on the bridge in the dark expecting to be hit over the head at any moment made us all very nervous and we had extra lookouts at hand, not to keep an eye open for other shipping but to keep an eye open for a mad mate. He had a special grudge against one of the engineers and tried to get down into the engine room to have a go at him. We eventually got him locked in his cabin and increased the ships speed to get to Rio as soon as possible. The last I saw of him was as he was led off the ship to a waiting ambulance as soon as we had docked and what ever became of the poor man I will never know. I do know that we all slept easier once he had left the ship. So the 2nd Mate took over the Chief Officer's job, I took over as 2nd Mate and the senior cadet became the 3rd, and it all seemed to work out quite well with us all giving each other a hand when a problem arose.

Rio, how does one explain or describe it. Even as you enter the harbour it takes your breath away with the harbour surrounded by towering hills all around and the Sugar Loaf Mountain standing tall and aloft. I went up it a few times and the view from the top is spectacular as you peer down onto the city then the far distance spreading into the Brazilian jungles. It is a hard climb to the top, but once there it's a vista you can never forget. The city itself is full of hustle and bustle, but once again it's the atmosphere that sends the blood rushing through your veins. The centre of the city is very modern with many office blocks and I used to love to just stroll around and mix with the crowd. Of course the other place to wander along is the Cocacabana Beach, just smiling at all the lovely girls in their very, very tiny bikinis. Once again they loved the British and we did our best to love them back!

One of the engineers was having a torrid affair, but it all came to an abrupt end. She, like the rest of the girls down there, was quite religious on Sundays, but for the rest of the week anything goes. In her flat over the bed she had a six foot crucifix attached to the wall and on this sad night when he lost her they were at it hammer and tongs when it fell of the wall and landed on top of them. She thought it was a sign from above and kicked him out and then, I was led to believe, she joined a convent. He was heart broken for at least half a day, but we took him down to the beach and he was soon in love, or lust as the case may be, and by the following evening he was smiling again. I was at Rio once during carnival week and the sight of those fantastic floats and costumes with the thousands of people there is something I will never forget. It was always with a sad heart that we had to let our ropes go and leave that wonderful place, but the bonus was that we would be returning in a few months time.

Down the coast we went and our next port was only 150 miles away and this was Santos. It was here that I celebrated my 21st birthday whilst we were at anchor for three weeks waiting for a berth. That was quite a day as my friend Les, the chief steward, had arranged a cocktail party for me after I came off anchor watch at 4 in the afternoon. All the other mates and engineers came as well as the passengers and they all had made me birthday cards, most of them on a filthy vein. 'Maggie the Snatch', my steward, had made a real beauty and when I opened it up there was the biggest condom I had ever seen stuck to it and a verse offering to make my birthday. I thanked him for the card and as for the other I told him to take a course in sex and travel, or to put it more crudely, ---- off! It was a terrific party and I think everyone was glad to break the monotony of sitting at anchor waiting to go alongside. I was put to bed at sometime and the Captain stood my watch that night, which was very noble of him as he was just about as drunk as the rest of us. Happy, happy days.

Santos was a lovely place and was well geared up for tourism with new hotels towering over the miles of unspoilt beaches and blue seas. It also had a good horse racing track of which a few of us keen punters went along some afternoons to donate our money to the bookies, but it was a good afternoon usually finishing up with a meal and then on to a couple of night clubs. Santos is the main port for Sao Paulo, the capital of Brazil, and is also the port that exports more coffee than anywhere else in the world, and that's a lot. On one trip myself and a friend flew up to Sao Paulo to see this city carved out of the jungle and to me it seemed out of place with its ultra modern buildings and modern factories and odd shaped statues scattered all over the place. I think that it hadn't come up to expectations and the Government had moved lots of workers into modern flats and houses, but the workers with the typical Brazilian attitude to life, hadn't taken to the modern life in a city and had returned back to their villages and small towns. The other problem was that the jungle had a habit of growing very quickly and it was an endless job to stop it from taking over again. Maybe it had the right idea. It was there that I saw the only big football match in my life and that was between Sao Paulo and its rivals Santos. The main man of the match was that great man Pele and some others in the Brazilian team and what they could do with that ball was terrific. They say that this country is football crazy, but compared to down there we are amateurs and with the sound of those drums beating the atmosphere was electric and when a goal was scored it was bedlam.

Once we had got rid of our cargo for Santos we then loaded the pallets of dreaded bananas and what was hiding in them, so for the next few days we were on snake and spider watch. We left Santos and followed the Brazilian coast line down south another 1,000 miles to the entrance to the River Plate and made for our next port which was Montevideo. As we sailed out of the south Atlantic and round Punta del Estre I always thought of Ajax, Achilles, Exeter and the great sea battle that took place in these waters against that mighty German battleship, the Graf Spee. When you enter the harbour at Montevideo there is a mass of old machinery on one of the quays and I enquired what it was and was told that it was part of the engines out of the Graf Spee, but I was never too convinced about that. One thing that I do know is that there are lots of Germans in Montevideo and I was led to believe that when the Graf Spee was eventually scuttled a vast amount of the crew didn't return home to carry on with the war, but settled here and who could blame them. Montevideo is the capital of Uruguay and has a population of about 1 million people, which gives you some idea of the size of the place. Unlike a lot of South American countries the Uruguay political system is quite stable hence it is a large financial centre with about seventy national banks in the centre of the city. It has some lovely nineteenth century architecture and has a large cathedral as well as a mass of large churches around each corner that you turn and in each square there is some statue or other. I found it a nice place, but funnily enough it doesn't have a large tourist trade which surprised me as the gardens scattered around the city are very attractive and there is a very pleasant drive along the River Plate called Rambla which goes for miles. As usual I had a great time ashore here and managed to fall in love, well sort of, with a very pretty girl who worked in one of the small bars in the town and I usually made my way back to the ship with the first shift of stevedores in the morning. She looked after me very well and life was very civilised. I became friendly with a chap at the shipping office and I spent many happy evenings with him and his wife at their home. On one trip he gave me a case of the local wine as well as a box of cigars and told me that the wine was one of the best produced in that area and that the cigars had a beautiful smell. Being a good son, I took my present back to my parents as a present for them. The bottles and cigars were passed on to friends of theirs and that was a big mistake as I believe that the wine was undrinkable and the cigars smelt and tasted of a wrestlers jock strap! Still, the thought was there and I didn't try to bring any more home. I liked Montevideo and the locals and always enjoyed my few days there. We stayed about a week to unload and then set off across the River Plate to Buenos Aires which was about 100 miles away. Once safely tied up alongside the passengers would leave the ship and be taken up to a lovely hotel and stay there while the ship finished unloading and would move up the Plate to a couple of other ports to start filling up with cargo for our return trip. This would take about fourteen days so the passengers could make Buenos Aires their base and explore the country from there. I remember that in those days the passengers were paying about £25 per week for the trip which couldn't be bad as they lived like lords aboard the ship with food fit for a king and then a two week stay at one of the top hotels in Buenos Aires. If I were offered a trip like that today, at the same price, you wouldn't see me for dust! As I have said earlier in the book I loved Buenos Aires and just to wander around the avenues, Cordaba, Corrientes, and the main one, De Julio, was always a joy especially at about 10 o'clock at night when everyone seemed to go for a stroll. To sit at one of the small bars at the side of the street and just watch the world go by was a pleasure and I have spent many a happy hour at this pursuit. Of course the other thing was to go to one of the many restaurants and a few bottles of wine and one of those huge juicy steaks. One night myself, Les the purser and the senior cadet were at one such place when we got chatting to three pretty girls who came across and joined us at our table. After a couple of hours, which was par for the course for a meal there, we found out that we had run up quite a bill and didn't have enough cash to settle the bill. Les the purser was in charge of monies aboard ship so he said he would go back to the ship and get us a sub. So whilst he returned to the ship myself and the cadet carried on drinking with the girls and prayed that he would return to that we wouldn't have to do the washing up for a week or at the worst get handed over to the police, which wasn't a very pleasant thought as a lot of people seemed to go missing in their hands. After an hour he thankfully returned and we all piled into a taxi and finished up at this fantastic hotel of which the whole of the front wall was on a swivel and opened up as a car approached. We all returned to the ship at about 07.00 the following morning worn out, but very happy. I have some very fond memories of Buenos Aires and it's a city I will never forget. The Chief Officer had married down there so as soon as we docked he was off home as fast as he could and none of us minded doing extra cargo watches and other duties as he was a well liked and respected man aboard the ship. When I left the sea he was still sailing as Chief Officer and I just hope that he got his own command in the end as he well deserved it. On one trip there I had a very nasty experience and, thank God, I never had another one like it. We were shifting from one loading berth to another and as I was 2nd Mate on this trip I was responsible for the after end of the ship when entering or leaving harbour or moving berths. I had three seamen with me to handle the ropes and wires and on this day one of the wire back springs broke and cut one of the seamans legs in half. The other seamen were being sick and one had passed out at the sight of all the blood and this leg held on by a few ligaments while we waited for the ambulance to take the poor man to hospital. I was as cool as a cucumber while all this was going on and asked the seamen if they were men or mice and couldn't they stand a bit of blood. When the injured man was safely ashore and on his way to the hospital I went to my cabin and poured myself a large Scotch, but all of a sudden my hands wouldn't keep still and I started shaking like a jelly and was as sick as a parrot as delayed shock set in. So much for being as cool as a cucumber and it took quite a time before I got my nerves back and could hold a glass without spilling it all over the place.

When our holds were empty we left Buenos Aires and moved up the Plate on a 250 mile trip inland which took us to a place called Sante Fe which was about 500 miles from the eastern coast, or nearly half way across Argentina. This was an interesting passage as the river got pretty narrow and you had more chance of hitting an overhanging tree than colliding with another ship. At one moment you could see for miles across pampas and then the next you were parting trees as we moved through dense jungle and trying to miss the many sand banks in the river. Most of the pilots that took us up river were very friendly and I had many long conversations with them as we did our "African Queen" bit. Once we got to Santa Fe it didn't have much to offer apart from a lot of humidity and dust and the town itself wasn't much to write home about. Like most of the towns in South America it had the usual cathedral and a church around every corner, but it was rather a bland place with not a lot to go ashore for. We only stayed there a few days while we loaded bone meal, hides and hoof and horns into the tween decks and a few hundred tons of grain into the lower holds. We couldn't load too much as it would put us too deep in the water and as the river was quite shallow in places we would run the risk of running aground. From Santa Fe we would wind our way back down the river to Rosario which was about 90 miles downstream and tie up at the grain berth which as I have described earlier was quite a way out of town which meant it was back to horse power to get us to the local bar and for those who had never been on a horse they soon learnt if they wanted a drink. We stayed there about five days whilst the local stevedores worked at their usual relaxed pace to load more grain into the bowels of the ship. When we had loaded a safe amount so that we wouldn't run aground on the 200 mile trip down river we cast off and headed once more for dear old Buenos Aires to fill the holds up for the return trip home. Just before we completed the loading the passengers would rejoin the ship and for the next few days we learnt all about their adventures ashore and all the places that they had visited. We nodded and showed enough interest to keep them happy whilst they related their stories, but at the same time thinking, "God I've heard all this before". Still, they were mostly nice people and it was pleasant to know that they had enjoyed themselves while ashore, and they were in kind paying our wages. So at last with the hatches covered it was time to leave Argentina and start to make our way back to England. We moved down the Plate and then turned into the South Atlantic heading in a northerly direction on our 2,000 mile trip along the Brazilian coastline to Bahia where we would pick up a few more hundred tons of cargo, also fuel and water. It was nice to get back into open waters and back to a routine instead of having to tie up every few days, also it was pleasant to feel a breeze and taste the salt in the air once more.

It was about a six day trip to Bahia and the weather was never too settled in this part of the ocean, but usually it was pretty good. I think that one of the nicest experiences that I can remember at sea was to stand on the bridge of the ship at night with a flat calm sea, the engines thumping away at a steady beat, the stars shining with a brilliance and the wake of the ship leaving a phosphorescent trail until it faded in the far distance astern. I think that those times it made me very much at peace with the world. During the day the passengers lounged around sunbathing or sometimes playing deck games and after dinner we organised something to stop them getting bored, such as bingo, bridge or some other form of entertainment. The crew were back to the task of chipping and painting again so that when we got back to

London the ship would look pretty smart for the shipping company, also for the next lot of passengers to join. Past Rio we steamed, with a lot of happy memories going around in our heads about the times ashore there, but at least we knew that we would be back in the not too distant future and more fun to look forward to. Our stay at Bahia was only a day whilst the few pallets of cargo was swung aboard and then we moved over to the oiling berth to take on more fuel for our crossing to the Canaries. As usual it was scorching hot there and we were glad that it was only a short stay before we were on the move again heading in a north easterly direction and a 2,700 mile trip. Over the equator we passed once more on our nine day cruise and life carried on in its steady daily routine with me standing my two watches each day from midday until 4 o'clock in the afternoon and then from midnight until 4 o'clock in the morning. When I talked to people about the hours they say what horrible times to work, but you got into a steady routine and it never bothered me and as I have said before, during those hours most aboard ship were asleep so it was very peaceful. I would sleep from when I came off the bridge at 04.00 until breakfast then turn in at about 8 o'clock in the evening until I got a call to take over the bridge at midnight. As 2nd Mate I was the main navigator aboard so I had to lay the course from port to port also keep the charts up to date so we didn't run into any new sunken hazards. To me it was fascinating and I loved navigation and to arrive at a spot within a few miles also at the time stated was always an achievement. I know that on one of the trips from Bahia to the Canaries I got caught out. We were about 120 miles from Las Palmas and I was on the bridge during the graveyard watch when I saw a flashing light ahead, but as there was no land around I couldn't work it out. I counted the flashes and it corresponded to the light at Las Palmas, so either my navigation was way out or the ship was doing about 30 knots during the past few hours! I hated doing it, but I called the Captain up on the phone and he came to the bridge. We double checked our D.R. position to make sure that we were where we should have been and it all seemed correct. After about half an hour the light couldn't be seen any more and we reckoned that it had been caused by a thing called super refraction where the light beam was being reflected off the cloud base and travelling to us 120 miles away. Nature is a funny thing. At Las Palmas we loaded a few pallets of tomatoes and our stay there was only for a few hours, so no shore leave for passengers or crew and we were then on our last leg of our trip. By now the weather had turned a bit chilly so away went our white uniforms and knees, and out came our blues, which always seemed very heavy and ungainly after so long in our whites. Past the coastline of Portugal and Northern Spain and then into the Bay of Biscay before turning round Ushant and the trip up the English Channel. Once in the Channel talk of leave came to the fore and an excitement hung over us, but the passengers started to become rather sad as their voyage was heading to a close and it would be back to a normal life in a few days time and then they just had the memories. Some of the mates and engineers would be staying for another trip before having leave, some would be going to another of the companies ships and the lucky ones would be going on leave. On my last trip to sea I am not sure what my feelings were. I knew that I would miss the comradeship of my fellow shipmates and the bond that exists at sea between us, also the great times that we had when we got ashore in foreign ports. I was not sorry to be having a full nights sleep instead of broken hours in my bunk. I'm not sure what I thought. Into the Thames the ship turned and then we winded our way up the river to Tilbury docks where the process of unloading started all over again and it would be a start of another trip, the continent, back to South America and return to Tilbury once again. As I have said earlier, I stayed with this shipping company until I left the sea in September 1964 and started my next career in the horse business, but I look back at the time that I tramped the oceans of the world and on reflection these were very happy times and I wouldn't have missed them for anything.

For the past twenty years or so I have lived on the Isle of Wight and often see Merchant shipping ploughing through the Solent. I get terribly nostalgic seeing these vessels and wonder, what cargo are they carrying, what is the next port of call, wouldn't I love to be standing once again on the bridge looking down at the bows of the ship as she cuts through the water. I suppose that I remember most of the good times when I was at sea and tend to forget the bad ones. The thing that does sadden me is the decline of the Merchant Navy and the amount of ships that actually fly the Red Ensign at the stern of the vessel. One day we might need the Merchant service again, but then it will be too late, as we wouldn't have enough ships and more important we wouldn't have men with experience to man them. This is a sad thought.